# MAN AND SIN

Understanding Biblical Anthropology
and Hamartiology

# Other Books by Dr. Arnold G. Fruchtenbaum

*A Passover Haggadah for Jewish Believers*
*An Historical and Geographical Study Guide of Israel: With a Supplement on Jordan*
*Ariel's Harmony of the Gospels*
*Faith Alone: The Condition of Our Salvation (An Exposition of the Book of Galatians and Other Relevant Topics)*
*God's Will & Man's Will: Predestination, Election, and Free Will*
*Ha-Mashiach: The Messiah of the Hebrew Scriptures*
*Israelology: The Missing Link in Systematic Theology*
*Jesus Was a Jew*
*The Feasts and Fasts of Israel – Their Historic and Prophetic Significance*
*The Footsteps of the Messiah: A Study of the Sequence of Prophetic Events*
*The Historical and Geographical Maps of Israel and Surrounding Territories*
*The Remnant of Israel: The History, Theology, and Philosophy of the Messianic Jewish Community*
*The Sabbath*
*What the Bible Teaches About Israel: Past, Present, and Future (An Abridged Version of Israelology: The Missing Link in Systematic Theology)*
*Yeshua: The Life of Messiah from a Messianic Jewish Perspective*, Volumes 1-4 & The Abridged Version

## Ariel's Bible Commentary Series:

*Biblical Lovemaking: A Study of the Song of Solomon*
*Judges and Ruth*
*The Book of Acts*
*The Book of Genesis*
*The Messianic Jewish Epistles (Hebrews, James, I & II Peter, Jude)*

## Ariel's Come and See Series:

*The Word of God: Its Nature and Content*
*What We Know About God: Theology Proper*
*Messiah Yeshua, Divine Redeemer: Christology from a Messianic Jewish Perspective*
*Ruach HaKodesh – God the Holy Spirit: Messianic Jewish Perspectives on Pneumatology*

# MAN AND SIN

## UNDERSTANDING BIBLICAL ANTHROPOLOGY AND HAMARTIOLOGY

ARNOLD G. FRUCHTENBAUM
TH.M., PH.D.

*Man and Sin*
*Understanding Biblical Anthropology and Hamartiology*
(Author: Arnold G. Fruchtenbaum, Th.M., Ph.D.)
Volume 6 in Ariel's "Come and See" Series
1ˢᵗ Edition © 2022 by Ariel Ministries

ISBN 978-1-951059-91-0
Library of Congress Control Number: 2022908580
REL101000 RELIGION / Messianic Judaism / Anthropology / Hamartiology / Creation / Evolutionism / Sin

Editor and Research Assistant: Christiane K. Jurik, M.A.
Cover illustration by Jesse and Josh Gonzales
We thank Jamie Howen for proofreading this book.

All rights reserved. No part of this publication may be translated, reproduced, distributed, or transmitted in any form or by any means, including photocopying, recording, or other electronic or mechanical methods, without the prior written permission of the publisher, except in the case of brief quotations embodied in critical reviews and certain other noncommercial uses permitted by copyright law. For permission requests, write to the publisher at the address below.

All Scripture quotations, unless otherwise noted, are from the *1901 American Standard Version* (Oak Harbor, WA: Logos Research Systems, Inc., 1994). However, the archaic language has been changed with one exception: The archaic *ye* has been retained to distinguish the second-person plural from the singular *you*. The words "Jesus" and "Christ" have been replaced with "Yeshua" and "Messiah" respectively.

Published by Ariel Ministries
P.O. Box 792507
San Antonio, TX 78279-2507
www.ariel.org

This volume of our Come and See series is dedicated to

JAMES TOUR.

For a time, Dr. Tour served on Ariel's Board of Directors. During those years, he provided valuable guidance and advice, for which we are still grateful. More recently, he was also very helpful to our editor in dealing with a chapter in this book that discusses creation versus evolution. A good deal of his help is reflected in that chapter. For these reasons, we dedicate this volume to him.

# Contents

PREFACE ........................................................................................................ 1

**PART 1: ANTHROPOLOGY**

**CHAPTER I: INTRODUCTION** ........................................................................ 5

**CHAPTER II: VIEWS THAT CONTRADICT THE BIBLICAL ACCOUNT** ............. 7

A. THREE CHURCH HERESIES ........................................................................ 7
B. EVOLUTIONISM ........................................................................................ 8
    1. The Influence of Evolutionism .......................................................... 9
        a. In General ................................................................................ 9
        b. Christian Variants of Evolutionism ........................................ 10
    2. Evolution ...................................................................................... 13
    3. The Case against the Theory of Evolution ................................... 13
        a. Its Unproven Assumptions .................................................... 14
        b. The Laws of Thermodynamics .............................................. 20
        c. Mutations ............................................................................. 28
        d. Dating Methods .................................................................... 30
    4. Conclusion .................................................................................... 37
C. QUESTIONS AND STUDY SUGGESTIONS ................................................. 41

**CHAPTER III: CREATIONISM** ..................................................................... 43

A. SCRIPTURES AND THE TERM *YOM* ....................................................... 43
B. THE CREATION ACCOUNT OF GENESIS 1:1–2:3 ..................................... 44
    1. Genesis 1:1 ................................................................................... 44
    2. Genesis 1:2 ................................................................................... 47
    3. Genesis 1:3-31 ............................................................................. 52
    4. The Sixth Day of Creation: Genesis 1:24-27 ................................ 53
    5. The Theological Implications ....................................................... 56
    6. The Completion of the Creative Work: Genesis 2:1-3 ................. 58
C. QUESTIONS AND STUDY SUGGESTIONS ................................................. 59

## CHAPTER IV: THE IMAGE OF GOD IN MAN ................................................ 61

- A. INTRODUCTION ................................................................................ 61
- B. SCRIPTURES .................................................................................... 63
- C. A PRELIMINARY DEFINITION OF THE IMAGE OF GOD ........................ 64
- D. THE COMPONENTS OF THE IMAGE OF GOD IN MAN ........................ 66
- E. THE CORRELATION BETWEEN THE IMAGE OF GOD AND REDEMPTION ... 67
- F. QUESTIONS AND STUDY SUGGESTIONS ............................................. 69

## CHAPTER V: THE COMPOSITION OF MAN ............................................... 71

- A. THE MATERIAL PART OF MAN .......................................................... 71
    1. The Transmission ..................................................................... 74
    2. The Designations ..................................................................... 75
    3. The Future ............................................................................... 76
    4. Summary ................................................................................. 76
- B. THE IMMATERIAL PART OF MAN ...................................................... 77
    1. The Origin ................................................................................ 77
    2. The Transmission ..................................................................... 78
        a. The Pre-existence of the Soul ............................................ 78
        b. The Doctrine of Creationism .............................................. 78
        c. The Doctrine of Traducianism ............................................ 81
    3. The Trichotomy of Man ........................................................... 82
    4. The Dichotomy of Man ............................................................ 85
    5. The Seven Facets of the Immaterial Part of Man .................... 88
        a. The Soul .............................................................................. 88
        b. The Spirit ............................................................................ 89
        c. The Heart ............................................................................ 91
        d. The Flesh ............................................................................ 93
        e. The Mind ............................................................................ 95
        f. The Will .............................................................................. 98
        g. The Conscience ................................................................ 100
- C. THE RELATIONSHIP BETWEEN THE MATERIAL AND THE IMMATERIAL .... 102
- D. QUESTIONS AND STUDY SUGGESTIONS ........................................... 104

## CHAPTER VI: THE FALL OF MAN ............................................................ 105

- A. THE STATE OF INNOCENCE ............................................................. 105
    1. Man's Unconfirmed Holiness ................................................. 105
    2. Man's Power of Contrary Choice ........................................... 106
    3. Man's Dominion over Creation .............................................. 107
    4. Man's Fellowship with God .................................................... 108
- B. MAN'S ORIGINAL ENVIRONMENT AND RESPONSIBILITIES .............. 108
- C. MAN'S PROBATIONARY PERIOD ..................................................... 110

| | |
|---|---|
| D. The Temptation | 111 |
|    1. The Progression | 112 |
|    2. The Areas of Temptation | 113 |
|    3. The Creation of Wrong Desires | 114 |
| E. The Reason for Such a Great Penalty | 115 |
| F. The Fall | 116 |
|    1. The Biblical Record | 116 |
|    2. The Self-Justification | 118 |
|    3. The Immediate Consequences | 118 |
|    4. The Dispensational Consequences | 120 |
| G. The Results | 120 |

**CHAPTER VII: THE BIBLICAL VIEW OF DEATH ................................. 123**

| | |
|---|---|
| A. The Origin of Death | 123 |
| B. Definition | 124 |
|    1. Physical Death | 124 |
|    2. Spiritual Death | 127 |
|    3. Eternal or Second Death | 127 |
| C. Death and the Work of the Messiah | 130 |
|    1. The Two Types of Resurrection | 130 |
|    2. The Different Types of Death Suffered by the Messiah | 133 |
| D. Death and the Believer | 134 |
|    1. The Messiah Conquered Death for the Believer | 135 |
|    2. The Messiah Causes Death for the Believer | 135 |
|    3. The Messiah Consecrated Death for the Believer | 137 |
|    4. Suicide | 138 |
| E. The Abolishment of Death | 141 |
|    1. The Abolishment of Physical Death for the Believer | 142 |
|       a. Old Testament Saints | 142 |
|       b. The Church Saints | 142 |
|       c. The Tribulation Saints | 144 |
|       d. The Millennial Saints | 144 |
|    2. The Abolishment of Physical Death for the Unbeliever | 144 |
| F. Questions and Study Suggestions | 146 |

**CHAPTER VIII: FREE AGENCY ................................................................. 149**

| | |
|---|---|
| A. Total Inability | 149 |
| B. Free Will | 150 |
| C. Conclusion | 152 |
| D. Questions and Study Suggestions | 152 |

## CHAPTER IX: THE GLORIFICATION OF MAN .................................................. 153

   A. THE RESURRECTION OF THE HUMAN BODY ............................................... 153
   B. THE NATURE OF THE RESURRECTED BODY ................................................. 155
   C. THE STATE OF GLORIFICATION ................................................................. 157
   D. THE RESTORATION OF MAN'S AUTHORITY ................................................ 159

## PART 2: HAMARTIOLOGY

## CHAPTER I: INTRODUCTION ........................................................................ 163

   A. ELEVEN HEBREW WORDS ........................................................................ 163
   B. SEVEN GREEK WORDS ............................................................................. 167
   C. TEN ENGLISH WORDS .............................................................................. 169

## CHAPTER II: WHAT IS SIN? ........................................................................... 171

   A. DEVELOPING A DEFINITION .................................................................... 171
   B. THE ESSENTIAL NATURE OF SIN ............................................................... 172

## CHAPTER III: THE ORIGIN AND UNIVERSALITY OF SIN .......................... 175

   A. WHERE AND HOW DID SIN BEGIN, AND WHO IT ITS AUTHOR? ................ 175
   B. SIN IS UNIVERSAL ................................................................................... 177

## CHAPTER IV: MAN'S ESTATE UNDER SIN .............................................. 181

   A. THE MEANING OF "LIVING UNDER SIN" ................................................. 181
   B. THE REMEDY FOR MAN'S ESTATE ........................................................... 182

## CHAPTER V: THE SIN NATURE — ORIGINAL SIN ................................... 183

   A. THE MEANING OF ORIGINAL SIN ............................................................ 183
   B. THE CONCEPT TAUGHT IN SCRIPTURE .................................................... 184
   C. THE TRANSMISSION OF THE SIN NATURE ............................................... 184
   D. THE PENALTY FOR THE SIN NATURE ....................................................... 185
   E. THE REMEDY FOR THE SIN NATURE ........................................................ 186

## CHAPTER VI: PERSONAL SIN ..................................................................... 187

   A. DEFINITION AND CLASSIFICATION .......................................................... 187
   B. THE CONCEPT TAUGHT IN SCRIPTURE .................................................... 188
   C. THE TRANSMISSION OF PERSONAL SIN .................................................. 189
   D. THE PENALTY FOR PERSONAL SIN .......................................................... 190
   E. THE REMEDY FOR PERSONAL SIN ........................................................... 191

## CHAPTER VII: IMPUTED SIN ..................................................... 193

A. DEFINITION ............................................................ 193
B. THE CONCEPT TAUGHT IN SCRIPTURE ...................................... 194
C. THE TRANSMISSION OF IMPUTED SIN ...................................... 194
D. THE PENALTY FOR IMPUTED SIN .......................................... 195
E. THE REMEDY FOR IMPUTED SIN .......................................... 196

## CHAPTER VIII: SIN IN THE BELIEVER'S LIFE ............................................ 197

A. THE CONCEPT TAUGHT IN SCRIPTURE ...................................... 197
B. THE RELATIONSHIP TO OTHER CATEGORIES OF SIN ......................... 198
C. THE PENALTY FOR SIN IN THE BELIEVER'S LIFE .......................... 199
D. THE REMEDY FOR SIN IN THE BELIEVER'S LIFE ........................... 200

## CHAPTER IX: THE FINAL TRIUMPH OVER ALL SIN .................................. 203

## CHAPTER X: THE NATURE OF THE LAW ............................................... 205

A. THE USAGES OF THE WORD "LAW" ......................................... 205
B. THE MEANING OF LAW .................................................. 207
C. TYPES OF LAW ........................................................ 208
D. THE PURPOSE OF THE LAW OF GOD ....................................... 209
E. THE BELIEVER AND THE LAW OF GOD ..................................... 210

## CHAPTER XI: QUESTIONS AND STUDY SUGGESTIONS .......................... 213

Man and Sin

# Preface

*What is Come and See?*

*Come and See* is a multi-volume collection of Messianic Bible studies transcribed from Dr. Arnold Fruchtenbaum's original radio broadcasts. For the book series, the manuscripts made from these transcripts were edited and expanded, and text based on his sermon notes was added.

Each study is a solid foundation upon which you can stand—a whiteboard from which you can teach or a podium from which you can preach the uncompromised truth to your congregation. This extensive collection is replete with expert knowledge of Hebrew, Greek, the Talmud, the history of the Jews, the geography of *Eretz Yisrael* (the land of Israel); a scholar's command of the Word; and the illumination of the *Ruach HaKodesh* (the Holy Spirit). *Come and See* will edify you in your personal devotion or small group Bible study regardless of which topic you choose.

*What Will You Discover in This Volume?*

Volume six of *Come and See* examines two areas of systematic theology: anthropology and hamartiology. Biblical anthropology is primarily concerned with the nature and origin of man. Hamartiology is the doctrine of sin.

Systematic theology is, of course, a logical development of what the Bible teaches about various subjects. The first main division is bibliology, which is the study of the Scriptures. We addressed the topic in volume one of *Come and See*, titled *The Word of God*. This is a logical beginning, since what we know about theology comes from the Scriptures themselves.

The second main division of systematic theology is theology proper, which is the doctrine of God. We addressed this topic in volume two of this series, titled *What We Know About God*. The study developed our understanding of God the Father and emphasized the deity, the theism, and the trinitarianism of God.

The third main division of systematic theology is Christology, also called "the doctrine of the Son" or "the doctrine of the Messiah." We covered this topic in volume three of our *Come and See* series, titled *Messiah Yeshua, Divine Redeemer: Christology from a Messianic Jewish Perspective*.

The fourth main division of systematic theology is pneumatology, also called "the doctrine of the Holy Spirit." We covered this topic in volume four of our *Come and See* series, titled *Ruach HaKodesh God the Holy Spirit: Messianic Jewish Perspectives on Pneumatology*.

The fifth main division of systematic theology is angelology, also called "the doctrine of angels." This topic was presented together with the two subtopics of Satanology and demonology in volume 5 of our *Come and See* series, titled *A Study of the Angelic Realm: Angelology, Satanology, and Demonology*.

*Questions and Study Suggestions for the Course*

At the end of many chapters, you will find questions and study suggestions that provide application relevant to the subject.

The goal of this collection is for disciples of *Yeshua* (Jesus) to grow in their faith and to live out their calling to make disciples.

# Part 1:
# Anthropology

Man and Sin

# Chapter I:
# Introduction

The English term "anthropology" originates in the Latin word *anthropologia* ("the study of mankind"). The Latin term is derived from the Greek words *anthrōpos* (meaning "humankind" or "humanity") and *logos* (meaning "thought," "study," or "meaning"). Hence, anthropology is the study of man.

The English term originated in the late sixteenth century, but only in the nineteenth century was it applied to the academic discipline that bears the name "anthropology." This discipline is usually separated into four branches: biological or scientific anthropology, archaeology, cultural anthropology, and linguistic anthropology. The primary focus of this book, however, is biblical anthropology, which is the study of man from a biblical viewpoint.

Biblical anthropology is mainly concerned with the nature of man. According to the Scriptures, man consists of spiritual and material aspects. Biblical anthropology takes a look at the relationship between these aspects. It seeks scriptural answers to questions such as:

- What does it mean to be human?
- What are the spiritual and material elements that make humanity unique in all of creation?
- Are human beings composed of two parts (body and soul-spirit) or three parts (body, soul, and spirit)?
- What does it mean that man is created in God's image?

Biblical anthropology is also concerned with man's relationship with God. It asks questions about the meaning and significance of the history of humanity as it is lived out before, with, and through God.

Biblical anthropology bases many of its premises on the creation account of Genesis 1–2. It presupposes the thought that God created humanity for Himself, which means that human beings exist for the purpose of having a relationship with this God. This connection was severed at the fall of man into sin, as described in Genesis 3. In order to determine how this broken relationship may be repaired, it is important to understand whether individuals are inherently good or evil. Biblical anthropology tries to answer this question.

It also deals with the question of life after death. Whether the soul continues to exist after death, either in the presence of God or separated from God, has a significant impact on people's understanding of their purpose in this world.

Finally, biblical anthropology enables human beings to see themselves through the eyes of God. When they gain a more complete understanding of their fallen nature, they develop a deeper appreciation of what God has accomplished through His plan of redemption.

In light of the depth of the questions biblical anthropology seeks to answer, biblical anthropology is clearly a worthwhile study. It is closely related to hamartiology, the doctrine of sin, which is covered in the second part of this book.

# Chapter II:
# Views that Contradict the Biblical Account

Before delving into the study of biblical anthropology, it is necessary to examine various views that contradict biblical teaching. The first three positions are church heresies. These will be mentioned only briefly. Evolutionism is the fourth perspective. It will be examined in greater detail and in a more scholarly manner that may seem overwhelming to some readers. If so, please proceed to the next chapter which details what the Bible teaches about the origin of man.

## A. Three Church Heresies

The first view is called gnosticism. It teaches that the *pneuma* of man (meaning his spirit, soul, or creative force) is part of the divine essence and is therefore incapable of sinning. The material part of man, on the other hand, is inherently sinful.

The second false view is that of semi-Pelagianism, a moderate form of the unbiblical doctrine of Pelagianism. Both Pelagianism and semi-Pelagianism deny the biblical doctrine of total depravity, which says that every part of man (his mind, will, emotions, and flesh) has been corrupted by sin. Semi-Pelagianism adds the human spirit to this list and teaches that it does not fall under the domination of sin.

The final view is annihilationism, which teaches that unbelievers will not experience an eternity of suffering in hell, but will instead be "extinguished" after death. It also teaches that by sin, man loses the divine element of *pneuma* and regains it by regeneration. Hence, only the regenerate live forever.

## B. Evolutionism

According to biblical anthropology, the origin of man lies with God. In contrast, biological or scientific anthropology is the study of the origin of life that excludes the possibility of any divine influence. In general, biblical anthropology and scientific anthropology contain some overlap, as both studies aim to understand cultures, human behaviors, languages, and history. However, the worldviews that come out of these explanations of the origin of life are vastly different.

In the following section, the origin of man will be viewed first from the naturalistic viewpoint, especially from the perspective of evolutionism. The viewpoint of creationism will be presented in the next chapter.

The term "evolutionism" refers to a philosophical and spiritual worldview. It is the philosophical interpretation of science within a naturalist framework. The terms "naturalistic" and "naturalism" refer to the belief that life is the outcome of a natural evolutionary process devoid of existential meaning or aim. According to evolutionism, human existence, like everything else, began as a cosmic accident. Humans are superior to all other creatures solely because they have developed to a greater degree of intellect that allows them to dominate other lifeforms and maximize their chance of survival. Upon death, the body decomposes into dust, and the person ceases to exist.

There are two schools of evolutionism: naturalistic evolutionism, which maintains that life began spontaneously; and theistic evolutionism, which maintains that God initiated the process.

## 1. The Influence of Evolutionism

### a. In General

In today's world, evolutionism has become part of an established framework for anthropology and zoology. As *The Encyclopedia Britannica* points out, evolution itself is a scientific working hypothesis, but one that has "no effective rival."[1]

Harlow Shapley (1885-1972), an American scientist and the former head of the Harvard College Observatory, noted that evolutionism eliminates the need to explain the origin of life in terms of the miraculous or the supernatural. When the conditions are favorable, life occurs, endures, and evolves automatically.[2]

The English evolutionary biologist and first director of UNESCO Sir Julian Huxley (1887-1975) summarized evolutionism in the following manner:

> The first point to make about Darwin's theory is that it is no longer a theory, but a fact. No serious scientist would deny the fact that evolution has occurred, just as he would not deny the fact that the earth goes around the sun... Darwinism removed the whole idea of God as the creator of organisms from the sphere of rational discussion. Darwin pointed out that no supernatural designer was needed; since natural selection could account for any known form of life, there was no room for a supernatural agency in its evolution... There was no sudden moment during evolutionary history when "spirit" was instilled into life, any more than there was a single moment when it was instilled into you... I think we can dismiss entirely all ideas of a supernatural overriding mind being responsible for the evolutionary process.[3]

---

[1] *The Encyclopedia Britannica: A Dictionary of Arts, Sciences, Literature and General Information*, Vol. II (Cambridge, UK: University Press, 1910), p. 109.

[2] See: Harlow Shapely, "Front Matter," *The Science News-Letter*, vol. 88, no. 1, 1965, p. 10.

[3] Sir Julian Huxley, "At Random: A Television Preview," in *Evolution After Darwin*, Vol. 3, Sol Tax, ed. (Chicago: University of Chicago Press, 1960), pp. 41-45.

This statement is the selling of a bill of goods. Especially in education, claims are made that something is absolutely true without providing proof. The fact that evolutionism is based on a theory rather than on objective truth is denied, ignored, or intentionally misrepresented.

### b. Christian Variants of Evolutionism

Evolutionism did not stop at the gates of evangelical churches, and various theories have developed from this worldview.

#### *(1) Theistic Evolution*

The first theory is referred to as "theistic evolution." Theistic evolution is the belief that God initiated evolutionary processes and continues to monitor them. The Word of God is seen as a collection of documents that contain truth. Yet, the uncovering of this truth is a matter of interpretation. As a result, the Bible must be interpreted anew for every era and for every situation.

#### *(2) Day-Age Theory*

The second hypothesis that developed from the influence of evolutionism upon evangelicals is called the "day-age theory." Like theistic evolutionists, those who hold to this view profess a certain allegiance to the Scriptures and attempt to harmonize the biblical account with the evolutionary scenario. The biblical text describes the creation of the universe and the earth in six days; evolutionists believe it took at least 4.5 billion years. The day-age theory is the mechanism that reconciles the two perspectives.

The crucial element in this attempted harmonization is the term "day" as it appears in Genesis 1. The Hebrew word for "day" is *yom*. Usually, this term refers to a 24-hour period. However, those who hold to the day-age theory cite II Peter 3:8, which states: *But forget not this one thing, beloved, that one day is with the Lord as a thousand years, and a thousand years as one day*. Based on this verse, the claim is made that the days of Genesis 1 should be understood as long eras that correspond to important periods of evolutionary geological history.

## *(3) Gap Theory*

The third hypothesis is referred to as the gap theory.[4] It claims that while the six days of creation were actual 24-hour periods, there was a gap of time between Genesis 1:1 and 1:2. The passage reads as follows:

> *[1]In the beginning God created the heavens and the earth. [2]And the earth was waste and void; and darkness was upon the face of the deep: and the Spirit of God moved upon the face of the waters.*

The Hebrew word for "was" in verse 2 is *hayetah*. While this term does indeed mean "was," it may also be translated as "became." This would render the verse as "The earth became (*hayetah*) waste and void (*tohu va-vohu*)." One reason to translate the verse this way is seen in Isaiah 45:18, which states that God did not create the earth as a wasteland: *For thus says Jehovah that created the heavens, the God that formed the earth and made it, that established it and created it not a waste, that formed it to be inhabited: I am Jehovah; and there is none else.*

Translating the Hebrew term *hayetah* in Genesis 1:2 with "became" suggests a process that led from one state (not waste and void) to another (*tohu va-vohu*). There are two interpretations of what led to this change and what happened in the period between Genesis 1:1 and 1:2. Some, such as this author, relate the account in these two verses to the fall of Satan described in Ezekiel 28:11-19. The fall of Satan resulted in God judging the earth by means of a flood. This divine judgment resulted in the earth becoming a wasteland. The temporal gap that followed God's judgment need not have been very long. Others claim that the gap lasted billions of years, the time they think is

---

[4] This theory is also known as gap creationism, ruin-restoration creationism, and restoration creationism.

needed to fit in the dinosaur age and to harmonize geological findings about the age of the earth with the Bible.

A concise survey[5] of the history of the gap theory reveals that this view did not develop at the time of Darwin. Rather, even early church writers noted that between Genesis 1:1 and 1:2 there was a period when the created world plunged into chaos,[6] and this was still a common view by the Middle Ages.[7] While certainly not the majority view, even some rabbis were willing to discuss this interpretation, as the following excerpt from the *Genesis Rabbah* shows:

> Rabbi Judah bar Simon said: it does not say, 'It was evening,' but 'And it was evening.' Hence we derive that there was a time-system prior to this. Rabbi Abbahu said: This teaches us that God created worlds and destroyed them, saying, 'This one pleases me; those did not please me.' Rabbi Pinhas said, Rabbi Abbahu derives this from the verse, 'And God saw all that He had made, and behold it was very good,' as if to say, 'This one pleases me, those others did not please me.'[8]

At the end of the 18th century and the beginning of the 19th century, the gap theory grew in popularity among theologians. A new understanding of geology was emerging at the time, concluding that the earth was much older than common Genesis interpretations and Bible-based flood geology would suggest. Christian scientists dominated the field of geology during this period. They saw science as a new source of authority and created what is now known as "natural theology." According to this doctrine, science was regarded as a second

---

[5] For a much longer survey, see: Ken Ham, *Six Days: The Age of the Earth and the Decline of the Church* (Green Forest, AR: Master Books, 2013), pp. 103-112.

[6] For example, see: Origen, *Homilies on Genesis and Exodus* (trans. by Ronald E. Heine; Washington, D.C.: The Catholic University of America Press, 2002), pp. 47-48.

[7] For the views of Hugh of Saint Victor (1096-1141), Thomas Aquinas (1225-1274), Denis Pétau (1583-1652), and Benedict Pereira (1536-1610), see: Arthur C. Custance, *Without Form and Void: A Study of the Meaning of Genesis 1:2* (Ontario, Canada: Doorway Publications, 1970), p. 28.

[8] *Bereishit Rabbah* 3:7; retrieved from www.sefaria.org.

revelation from God. Scripture and nature were both places where God's Word could be found. As a result, these realms must not conflict with one another. The gap theory enabled theologians to reconcile their faith in the Bible with science's new authority. Today, natural theology is based exclusively on observed facts and personal experience, apart from any divine revelation.[9]

## 2. Evolution

The term "evolution" is commonly defined as a one-way process that is irreversible in time. This process is capable of producing novelties, a greater variety, and a higher degree of organization within matter. It turns that which is simple into something more differentiated, complex, and integrated. This is true for both organic and inorganic materials.

Biological evolution is the process of change through which the primordial cell is said to have developed into the diversity of life that exists today. Natural selection and neutral drift are thought to be the main factors behind this process. The expression "neutral drift" refers to the small genetic changes that are passed from parent to offspring. By themselves, these small changes do not lead to a mutation. They are "neutral." But eventually, after a few or many such small genetic modifications, a mutation occurs, positive or negative. The change towards complexity is continuous.

## 3. The Case against the Theory of Evolution

This is not a textbook on the science of evolution but a book that deals with the biblical view of the origin of man. Hence, after introducing several general objections to the evolutionary theory, it will make the biblical case against evolution.

---

[9] See: Tom McIver, "Formless and Void: Gap Theory Creationism," *Creation/Evolution*. Issue XXIV, Vol. 8, Number 3, Fall 1988, pp. 1-24.

## a. Its Unproven Assumptions

The British organic chemist and young-Earth creationist Arthur Ernest Wilder-Smith (1915-1995) provided the following critical definition of the theory of evolution:

> They assume that primitive life, or the primitive cell, was so simple that it... arose by pure chance. In some primitive ocean the correct concentrations of inorganic salts, ammonia, carbon dioxide, etc., arose, so that by chance some amino acids were formed. These then polymerized into polypeptides[10] which combined with one another by chance to give the first primitive molecule. Protein is today a prerequisite for life, and once we have a ready-made protein, life could start to "ride" upon it. Thus, primitive biogenesis[11] (archebiopoiesis)[12] is postulated to have "occurred". For the thorough-going Darwinist the only creator at work in this whole process is chance variation and selection working over millions of years in a favorable environment.[13]

Nowadays, the theory to which Wilder-Smith was reacting critically has been superseded by the RNA World Hypothesis. This hypothesis suggests that, approximately four billion years ago, before living cells, the genetic code, and the gene-protein cycle ever existed, chains of a chemical called RNA began forming naturally. Once formed, some of these chains demonstrated the ability to function as enzymes and even evolved by making copies of themselves with minor, accidental modifications.

---

[10] Polypeptides are linear organic polymers consisting of a large number of amino-acid residues bonded together in a chain, forming part of (or the whole of) a protein molecule.

[11] Biogenesis is the development of living organisms or a theory of the same.

[12] Archebiopoiesis is the original or first formation of a living organism from lifeless matter. It is the first generation of life.

[13] A. E. Wilder-Smith, Man's Origin, *Man's Destiny: A Critical Survey of the Principles of Evolution and Christianity* (Chicago, IL: Harold Shaw Publishers, 1969), pp. 34-35.

In its purest form, the RNA World Hypothesis states that RNA came first, followed by DNA and proteins. In the past fifty years, this hypothesis has gone from speculation to a widely held belief.

However, in its purest form, the hypothesis is not largely accepted. The majority of scientists now believe that RNA, DNA, small proto-proteins, and even lipids have always coexisted. While these scientists do not doubt that RNA played a crucial role in the early development of life, the complexity of RNA and DNA nucleotides calls into question the notion that RNA was the first truly replicating and evolving chemical system. As a result, alternatives to the "RNA first" hypothesis are being explored.

The theory of evolution is not concerned with the origin of life, but with the mechanism that drives the changes necessary for the continuation of the evolutionary process from the first life onward. In the above quote, Wilder-Smith emphasized the fact that evolution relies on chance. By chance, a mutation occurs. Some of these mutations give the possessor an advantage in the struggle for existence. The result is that the possessor of the mutation becomes more numerous and has more offspring than the non-possessor. Consequently, different varieties develop by chance mutations out of a single standard simplicity. Again, nowadays, the concept of mutation has been supplanted by "neutral drift."

This process is continuous, as is the struggle for existence. In the words of Charles Darwin, only the fittest survive this struggle. The biological concept of fitness is defined as reproductive success and is best understood in Darwinian terms as the survival of the form that leaves the most copies of itself in subsequent generations. The mechanism at work here is called "natural selection." It is the process by which organisms that are more adapted to their surroundings have a better chance of survival and of producing more offspring. Natural selection is considered the most important driving force in evolution. Without the struggle for survival, there can be no natural selection and no upward development in evolution. This upward development leads from primitive microspheres and the first cell-like structures (known as coacervates) to "the evolutionary family tree, as it is conceived by Darwinians to be today. The upward development and formation of present species is supposed to have required millions of years."[14]

The theory of evolution bases much of its premises on unproven assumptions. This point was expertly brought out by Gerald Allan Kerkut (1927-2004), Professor of Physiology and Biochemistry at the University of Southampton. It must be noted that the "science" evolves so quickly that opinions such as Kerkut's may seem outdated and at times address theories that have long been debunked by the scientific community itself. However, Kerkut made some points that may be general enough to apply even to today's hypotheses.

Kerkut was not an anti-evolutionist, but in his book *Implications of Evolution*, he referred to seven such evolutionary assumptions that lack sufficient evidentiary support:

> There are... seven basic assumptions that are often not mentioned during discussions of evolution. Many evolutionists ignore the first six assumptions and consider only the seventh. The first assumption is that nonliving things gave rise to living material, that is, that spontaneous generation occurred. The second assumption is that spontaneous generation occurred only once. The other assumptions all issue from this second one. The third assumption is that viruses, bacteria, plants, and animals are all interrelated. The fourth assumption is that the protozoa [unicellular eukaryotes that are either free-living in the environment or parasitic on plants or animals] gave rise to the metazoa [group of multicellular animals]. The fifth assumption is that the various invertebrate phyla are interrelated. The sixth assumption is that the invertebrates gave rise to the vertebrates. The seventh assumption is that the vertebrates and fish gave rise to the amphibia, the amphibia to the reptiles, and the reptiles to the birds and mammals. Sometimes this is

---

[14] A. E. Wilder-Smith, *The Natural Sciences Know Nothing of Evolution* (Costa Mesa, CA: T.W.F.T. Publishers, 1981), p. 2.

expressed in other words, that is, that the modern amphibia and reptiles had a common ancestral stock, and so on.[15]

Kerkut continued his discussion of evolution under the premise that most evolutionists believe in the truthfulness of all seven assumptions. For them, these assumptions form the general theory of evolution, even though they are not experimentally verifiable. To believe in them means to believe that a certain series of events has occurred in the past. Even if it were possible to recreate some of these events under current conditions, it would not imply that they must have occurred in the past. All it would show is that such a change is possible. In truth, scientists cannot bring about such a change at all. Instead, they must rely on limited circumstantial evidence to support their assumptions.

After this critical reflection on the trust in the seven assumptions, Kerkut continued:

> We are on somewhat stronger ground with the seventh assumption, namely that the fish, amphibia, reptiles, birds and mammals are interrelated. There is fossil evidence to help us here, though many of the key transitions are not well documented and we have as yet to obtain a satisfactory method of dating the fossils. The dating is of the utmost importance, for until we find a reliable method of dating the fossils, we shall not be able to tell if the first amphibians arose after the first choanichthian[16] or whether the first reptile arose from the first amphibian The evidence we have at present is insufficient to allow us to decide the answer to these problems.[17]

Kerkut argued that to some extent, many modern evolutionists seem to be basing their views on the evolution of all forms of life from

---

[15] G. A. Kerkut, *Implications of Evolution* (New York, NY: Pergamon, 1960), pp. 8-9.

[16] The term "choanichthyes" is used by some zoologists to group lobe-finned fish and lungfish. Members of this group or subclass were thought to share functional lungs, external and internal nares (nostrils), and narrow-based, paired fins with fleshy lobes.

[17] Kerkut, *Implications of Evolution*, p. 153.

simple to complex solely "on the nature of specific and intraspecific evolution."[18] He concludes that it would be premature, "not to say arrogant,"[19] to make dogmatic claims about the evolution of major animal branches. To the student of the future,

> Everything will seem simple and straightforward once it has been explained. Why, then, cannot we see some of these solutions now?... One reason is often that an incorrect idea of "fact" is accepted and takes the place of the correct one... Most students become acquainted with many of the... concepts in biology while still at school and at an age when most people are, on the whole, uncritical. Then when they come to study the subject in more detail, they have in their minds several half-truths and misappraisal of the situation. In addition, with the uniform pattern of education most students tend to have the same sort of educational background and so in conversation and discussion they accept common fallacies and agree on matters based on these fallacies...
>
> This theory... can be called the General Theory of Evolution and the evidence that supports it is not sufficiently strong to allow us to consider it as anything more than a working hypothesis... The answer (to the problem of evolution) will be found by future experimental work and not by dogmatic assertions that the General Theory of Evolution must be correct because there is nothing else that will satisfactorily take its place.[20]

Summarizing Kerkut's points, one may conclude that it is a matter of faith to trust the seven evolutionary assumptions. It is also a matter of faith to trust that the findings of evolutionary science are true. The American biologist and professor at Princeton University John T. Bonner (1920-2019) came to a similar conclusion when he wrote the following about Kerkut's work:

---

[18] Ibid., p. 155.
[19] Ibid, p. 156.
[20] Ibid., pp. 156-157.

> This is a book with a disturbing message; it points to some unseemly cracks in the foundations. One is disturbed because what is said gives us the uneasy feeling that we knew it for a long time deep down but were never willing to admit this even to ourselves. It is another one of those cold and uncompromising situations where the naked truth and human nature travel in different directions. The particular truth is simply that we have no reliable evidence as to the evolutionary sequence of invertebrate phyla. We do not know what group arose from what other group or whether, for instance, the transition from protozoa occurred once, or twice, or many times... We have all been telling our students for years not to accept any statement on its face value but to examine the evidence, and, therefore, it is rather a shock to discover that we have failed to follow our own sound advice.[21]

The Ukrainian-American geneticist and evolutionary biologist Theodosius Dobzhansky (1900-1975) wrote the following review of Kerkut's book:

> He argues, correctly of course, that we do not know exactly when and how life arose from nonliving matter... and, indeed, a vast amount of work remains to be done. The basic conclusion of the author is, however, something else—since we cannot yet reconstruct in all details the phylogeny of the animal kingdom, therefore evolution is not "proven"! This is a confusion of two distinct problems: we may be sure that life (or, for that matter, the Cosmos) had a history, but it does not follow that we know all the events of which these histories are composed with their respective dates. The author has been wise not to suggest any alternatives to the theory of evolution.[22]

Wilder-Smith, Kerkut, and Dobzhansky all wrote in the 1960s and 70s. The bibliographical data of their works may be dated, but some of

---

[21] John T. Bonner, "Perspectives," *American Scientist*, Vol. 49, no. 2, 1961, p. 240.

[22] Theodosius Dobzhansky, "Implications of Evolution," *Science*, 17 Mar 1961, Vol. 133, Issue 3455, p. 752.

their analyses are not. Creationists and evolutionists base their beliefs on the same evidence, the same facts. One group believes in the Creator God, the other denies His existence. It is the foundational and presuppositional beliefs undergirding these two polar-opposite worldviews that lead the respective scientists down the path to their final interpretations. For evolutionists, the stakes are high. The very idea of a Creator may frighten them because it raises an obvious question: "Will I submit to this Creator?" As theologian and publisher Mark R. Rushdoony pointed out in a foreword to *The Mythology of Science*,

> The "mythology" of modern science is its religious devotion to the myth of evolution. Evolution so expresses or coincides with the contemporary spirit that its often-radical contradictions and absurdities are never apparent, in that they express the basic presuppositions, however untenable, of everyday life and thought. In evolution, man is the highest expression of intelligence and reason, and such thinking will not yield itself to submission to a God it views as a human cultural creation, useful, it at all, only in a cultural context.[23]

## b. The Laws of Thermodynamics

The laws of thermodynamics have been proven scientifically. All physical, biological, and chemical processes known to man are subject to these laws. In simplest terms, they dictate the specifics for the movement of heat and energy and describe energy relationships for the entire known universe. Science often speaks of four laws of thermodynamics, but as will be seen, only two have a meaningful connection to creationism.

**The First Law of Thermodynamics** is also known as the conservation of energy. It states that energy can neither be created nor destroyed. In physics, energy is defined as the ability to perform work. Energy exists in different forms. From mechanics, we know kinetic and

---

[23] Rousas J. Rushdoony, *The Mythology of Science* (Vallecito, CA: Ross House Books, 2009), n. p.

potential energy, and thermodynamics adds internal or thermal energy to the mix. The first law describes how energy is converted between different forms and how it is transported in form of heat and work.

While the first law describes the conversion of work into heat and vice versa, it cannot distinguish between possible and impossible processes. Nevertheless, thermodynamic processes are constrained in many ways. One example is that hot coffee will always give up its heat to the cooler environment. It will get cold by itself, but the process will never reverse. A cup of coffee will never become hot on its own. Another example is mixtures. Without an external force, they cannot be separated.

These restrictions are formulated in **the Second Law of Thermodynamics**, which states that although there is a constant amount of energy in a given system that is simply transforming into different states, that energy becomes less useful as it does so. An example is water flowing from the top of a mountain into a valley. Its movement generates kinetic energy, but eventually, the water merges with a larger body of water, such as the ocean. It is still present, but it is no longer useful in providing energy on land.

The second law introduces a new quantity called "entropy." In physics, entropy is the measure of a system's disorder. The entropy of a system increases as it transitions from a more ordered, organized, and planned state to one that is more disordered, dispersed, and unplanned. The greater the disorder in a system, the higher is its entropy. According to the Law of Entropy, the universe as a whole is inevitably moving toward a more disordered, unplanned, and disorganized state.

Entropy can only be created, but not destroyed. It can only increase, not decrease unless acted upon by an external force. It is a quantity that can be used to characterize the irreversibility of a process. So, in the case of the hot coffee that transfers its energy to the cooler environment, this process is irreversible. Unless one reheats the coffee in the microwave oven, it will not get hot again.

The unusual feature of life, even a single cell, is that it has high energy but low entropy. Most things with low entropy are also low energy.

Probability and entropy are closely related. This relationship may be explained by the following scenario: A volume contains gas particles that are separated from another volume of the same size by a partition wall. When the partition is removed, the gas particles disperse throughout the now combined volumes. If one waits long enough, it is reasonable to expect that the gas particles will be evenly distributed throughout the volume. The most probable distribution is a uniform distribution. On the other hand, the probability of all particles reassembling in their original volume is extremely low.

The truth of the Second Law of Thermodynamics, or the Law of Entropy, can be proven both experimentally and theoretically. The American physiologist Harold Francis Blum (1899-1980) explains what this means for the theory of evolution:

> A major consequence of the second law of thermodynamics is that all real processes go toward a condition of greater probability. The probability function generally used in thermodynamics is entropy... The second law of thermodynamics says that left to itself, any isolated system will go toward greater entropy, which also means toward greater randomization and greater likelihood.[24]

Roger Lewin, a British science writer and evolutionist, expresses the difficulty of entropy for the theory of evolution this way: "One problem biologists have faced is the apparent contradiction by evolution of the second law of thermodynamics. Systems should decay through time, giving less, not more, order."[25] All things become more disorganized, more random. Evolution requires the exact opposite. It requires the increase of order, organization, size, and complexity.

---

[24] Harold F. Blum, "Perspectives in: Evolution," *American Scientist*, Vol. 43, no. 4, 1955, p. 595.

[25] Roger Lewin, "A Downward Slope to Greater Diversity," *Science*, Volume 217, Sep 24, 1982, p. 1239.

According to evolutionism, all matter in the universe initially was condensed in a tiny sphere. That sphere exploded, and over time, nonliving carbon, hydrogen, and nitrogen particles organized themselves into more complex, more energy-rich, and less chaotic forms. Even if this theory were true, it does not explain the origin of that tiny sphere.

Alan Guth, a cosmologist and physics professor at the Massachusetts Institute of Technology, explained the problem by stating that "inflation itself takes a very small universe and produces from it a very big universe. But inflation by itself does not explain where that very small universe came from."[26] He further states, "A proposal that the universe was created from empty space is no more fundamental than a proposal that the universe was spawned by a piece of rubber. It might be true, but one would still want to ask where the piece of rubber came from."[27]

Commenting on the thermodynamic impossibility of the spontaneous formation of life in a letter to the editors of the well-respected journal *American Scientist*, George Stravropoulos writes:

> Under ordinary conditions, no complex organic molecule can ever form spontaneously, but will rather disintegrate, in agreement with the second law. Indeed, the more complex it is, the more unstable it will be, and the more assured, sooner or later, is its disintegration. Photosynthesis and all life processes, and life itself, cannot yet be understood in terms of thermodynamics or any other exact science, despite the use of confused or deliberately confusing language.[28]

Blum used the Second Law of Thermodynamics to illustrate how the nonliving world places limits on the theory of evolution. He explained:

---

[26] As quoted in Fred Heeren, *Show Me God: What the Message from Space is Telling Us About God* (Wheeling, IL: Day Star Publications, 1995), p. 148.

[27] As quoted in Moreno Dal Bello, *A Reason and Purpose for Everything: The Existence of God, Who He Is, and How He Saves* (Lulu, 2017), p. 45.

[28] George P. Stravropoulos, Letters to the Editors Section, *American Scientist*, Vol. 65, Nov.–Dec. 1977, p. 675.

> Let us examine the possibility of the spontaneous formation of protein molecules from a non-living system. We may assume, for purposes of argument, that, in the course of chemical evolution, there had already come into existence a mixture containing a great quantity of various amino acids... The free energy change for the formation of peptide bonds is such that, at equilibrium, about one percent of the amino acids would be joined together as dipeptides, granting the presence of appropriate catalysts. The chances of forming tripeptides would be about one hundredth that of forming dipeptides, and the probability of forming a polypeptide of only ten amino acids as units would be something like $10^{-20}$. The spontaneous formation of a polypeptide of the size of the smallest known proteins seems beyond all probability. This calculation alone presents serious objections to the idea that all living systems are descended from a single protein molecule, which was formed as a "chance" act. ...
>
> The riddle seems to be: How, when no life existed, did substances come into being which, today, are absolutely essential to living systems, yet which can only be formed by those systems? ...
>
> If proteins were reproduced as they must have been, if living systems were to evolve [from nonliving systems], free energy had to be supplied. The source of this energy is a fundamental problem we must essentially face. ...
>
> The quanta of sunlight are inadequate to supply the energy necessary to forward this endergonic reaction [photosynthesis].[29]

Commenting on Blum's observations, Wilder-Smith writes:

> The fundamental problem with which Dr. Blum is wrestling is that of building a protein metabolic motor to support life before life was present to build it... How was the motor to extract energy from the environment built before life processes had arisen to build it? Once a motor (enzyme metabolic system) is present, it

---

[29] Harold F. Blum, *Time's Arrow and Evolution* (Princeton University Press, 1968), p. 158-166.

can easily supply the free energy necessary to build more and more motors, that is, to reproduce. But the basic problem is: How do we account for the building of the first complex enzymatic protein metabolic motor to supply energy for reproduction and other cell needs? ... Once the motor has been designed, fabricated and is running, the life processes work perfectly well on the principles of the known laws of thermodynamics.[30]

While Wilder-Smith may have oversimplified things in his response, there is an element of truth that is worthy of consideration. For those who believe in evolution, the only logical possibility for the origin of the matter and energy comprising the universe is that they spontaneously generated. They caused themselves to exist.

To finish the section on the four laws of thermodynamics, the third law indicates that entropy approaches zero as absolute temperature drops to zero. In other words, there is the possibility of temporarily decreasing entropy. However, the second law will win eventually. The fourth law is often called the "Zeroth Law" because it builds the foundation of the other laws. Stated simply, it indicates that thermodynamic equilibrium is associative: If two systems are each in thermal equilibrium with a third system, then they are also in equilibrium with each other. Thermal equilibrium means that when two systems are brought into contact with each other and are separated by a thermally permeable barrier, there is no heat transfer from one system to the other.

The laws of thermodynamics and the theory of evolution are opposites and cannot both be true. There is no doubt that thermodynamics is true. Consequently, the theory of evolution must be wrong.

Some evolutionists have proposed exceptions to the Second Law of Thermodynamics to allow evolution to proceed despite the problem of entropy. These scientists also claim that the synthesis of molecules becomes more likely if given enough time. Wilder-Smith counters these arguments by stating:

---

[30] Wilder-Smith, *Man's Origin*, pp. 61-62.

> The longer the molecules are exposed to random forces, the wider will become their random distribution and the fewer chances of forming an ordered protein or nucleic acid molecule out of nonliving random molecules. Increasing reaction time may increase the chances of synthesis. But according to the laws we have just been studying, increasing reaction time in reversible reactions will also increase still more the possibility of degradation (randomness) of already synthesized molecules, that is, if their entropy is lower than that of the starting materials. It is so easy to forget that the possibility of decomposition in reversible reactions increases with time just as the chance of synthetic processes does.[31]

Commenting on the issue of time needed in the process of the formation of life, Blum noted:

> I think if I were rewriting this chapter (of the origin of life) completely, I should want to change the emphasis somewhat. I should want to play down still more the importance of the great amount of time available for highly improbable events to occur. One may take the view that the greater time elapsed the greater should be the approach to equilibrium, the most probable state, and it seems that this ought to take precedence in our thinking over the idea that time provides the possibility for the occurrence of the highly improbable.[32]

Some have made the following counter-argument to the creationists' position regarding the Second Law of Thermodynamics: This law is irrelevant to evolution because the earth is not an isolated system since the sun is constantly pumping in more energy. They claim that free energy decreases entropy. But for this principle to work, energy must be supplied to the molecules before entropy can be reduced to increasing complexity, and the source of free energy must carry out this orderly process of molecular basis in the archebiopoiesis (the original

---

[31] Wilder-Smith, *Man's Origin, Man's Destiny*, p. 67.

[32] Blum, *Time's Arrow and Evolution*, p. 178.

or first formation of a living organism from lifeless matter). Wilder-Smith explained it this way:

> Solar energy, even though it may bathe nonliving matter, is not available to it for synthesis of the type in which we are interested. A complex metabolic (protein) motor is a necessary intermediate in making solar energy available. Chlorophyll (chloroplasts) function as just such a motor but is far too complex to have arisen by chance processes from nonliving matter.[33]

In conclusion, everything is subject to the law of deterioration or decay, including genetic material. Throughout the universe, entropy is increasing, and chaos is continuously replacing order (with local exceptions caused by local energy expenditures). However, measuring these processes will never give us information about the origin of life and matter.

Genetic degeneration in humans, which is well documented, is the antithesis of evolution. Retired Cornell University Research Geneticist John C. Sanford notes in an article published on the Internet:

> The lifespan data strongly supports the historicity and veracity of the Bible, and in particular, the book of Genesis... The lifespan data indicate that the extreme longevity of the early Patriarchs was real, and that the rapid decline of longevity after the Flood was real. This supports the Biblical perspective of on-going degeneration since the Fall. In light of recent scientific findings, the documented decline in longevity is best understood in terms of mutation accumulation and genetic entropy... The drastic decline in longevity began very specifically at the time of the Flood. This strongly supports the reality of a supernatural, cataclysmic world-changing flood, not an ordinary or local flood... The declining

---

[33] Wilder-Smith, *Man's Origin, Man's Destiny*, p. 71.

longevities strongly indicate that evolution is going the wrong way, and that the evolutionary timeline is not viable.[34]

### c. Mutations

One argument that is often brought up by evolutionists in support of their position comes from observable change. Evolutionists point to cases in which a mutation has benefited a creature in the struggle for survival. Some of these changes can be observed in the laboratory or in the natural world. Mutations are changes in the sequence of an organism's DNA and are said to be the primary source of organismal diversity. Pointing to the fundamental importance of mutations for the theory of evolution, Bonner explains:

> Since mutation means a chemical change in the gene structure, all progressive advancements must ultimately be by mutation, and all that can be done by recombination is to shuffle what is given by mutation. Gene mutation provides the raw material for evolution, and recombination sets this material out in different ways so that selection may be furthered by being provided with a whole series of possible arrangements.[35]

An example of an observable mutation is the following: Italian researchers studying the population of Burkina Faso at the turn of the twenty-first century discovered a protective effect associated with a variant of hemoglobin called HbC. Individuals carrying one copy of this gene are twenty-nine percent less likely to contract malaria, while those carrying two copies are ninety-three percent less likely. This hemoglobin mutation is undoubtedly beneficial to the people of Burkina Faso, but does it prove evolution?

Mutations are what is said to drive evolution. They would be needed to add information so that molecules can turn into a man over

---

[34] John C. Sanford, et al. *Genetic Entropy Recorded in the Bible?* Feed My Sheep Foundation, https://www.kolbecenter.org/wp-content/uploads/2014/07/Genetic-Entropy-Recorded-in-the-Bible.pdf.

[35] John Tyler Bonner, *The Ideas of Biology* (Mineola, NY: Dover Publications, 2002), n. p.

time. Without mutations, the theory of evolution has no leg to stand on. James F. Crow, an expert on radiation and mutation, notes:

> The general picture of how evolution works is now clear. The basic raw material is the mutant gene. Among these mutants most will be deleterious, but a minority will be beneficial. These few will be retained by... the sieve of natural selection. As the British statistician R. A. Fischer has said, natural selection is "a mechanism for generating an exceedingly high level of improbability." It is [James Clerk] Maxwell's famous demon superimposed on the random process of mutation. Despite the clarity and simplicity of the general idea, the details are difficult and obscure.[36]

This statement is fairly descriptive of the evolutionary theory. True mutations do occur and may result in a permanent change of species because genetic material was recombined due to "a mutagenic chemical or some other disorganizing agent."[37] However, observable mutations are typically neutral, meaning they have no effect on the outcome or meaning of the genetic code. More often, they result in the loss or corruption of information, as Crow points out:

> Mutations and mutation rates have been studied in a wide variety of experimental plants and animals, and in man. There is one general result that clearly emerges: almost all mutations are harmful.[38] The degree of harm ranges from mutant genes that kill their carrier, to those that cause only minor impairment... [A] mutation is a random change of a highly organized, reasonably smoothly functioning living body. A random change in the highly integrated

---

[36] James F. Crow, "Ionizing Radiation and Evolution," *Scientific American*, vol. 201, no. 3, 1959, p. 142.

[37] Henry Madison Morris, *The Twilight of Evolution* (Grand Rapids, MI: Baker Book House, 1963), p. 43.

[38] An example of a beneficial mutation is seen in bacteria that survived the insult of an antibiotic. The mutant that survived reproduces and shares its DNA with other bacteria giving others, even outside its own offspring, the antibiotic resistance. So, mutations have been observed to be organism beneficial.

system of chemical processes which constitute life is almost certain to impair it.[39]

Hence, instead of the needed "uphill" change, mutations cause "downhill" changes that indicate a loss of information. Mutations are subject to the Second Law of Thermodynamics, and the natural tendency is toward a greater degree of disorder and randomness. Furthermore, change has only been observed within species. Mutations that reach across species (such as in the case of a mule) are not being passed on because the mutant does not reproduce. These facts contradict the theory that from one molecule evolved the variety of plants, animals, and human beings we see today.

### d. Dating Methods

There are two dating methods that evolutionists generally assume to be reliable and true.

The first method is known as **radiometric (or C-14) dating**. Scientists use this method to estimate the ages of rocks, fossils, and the earth. What is tested is the amount of carbon in the rock or fossil. The greater the amount of a certain carbon isotope in an item, the younger the item is.

In 1960, Willard Frank Libby (1908-1980) received the Nobel Prize in Chemistry for his role in the 1949 development of this new method of dating. He experimented on a piece of wood from the coffin of Djoser, an Egyptian pharaoh of the Third Dynasty. The tests revealed that the wood was 4,600 years old, and thus the pharaoh and his pyramid were dated. It was a watershed moment in archaeology. Until then, the only way to tell which structure was older or younger was to compare styles. C-14 dating was a game changer: It established a definite age. That was the theory. Chemically, radiocarbon dating is based on the fact that there are three naturally occurring carbon isotopes on Earth. Carbon-12 is the most stable form and accounts for the

---

[39] James F. Crow, "Genetic Effects of Radiation," *Bulletin of the Atomic Scientists*, Vol. 14, January 1958, pp. 19-20.

majority of all carbon. Carbon-13 is also stable and accounts for one percent of the total. Carbon-14 is a radioactive isotope that is unstable. It is only found in trace amounts. It is formed in the upper atmosphere when cosmic rays collide with nitrogen. The C-14 must then enter the biosphere from the upper atmosphere. It does so through photosynthesis. As a result, radiocarbon enters the food chain. Radiocarbon is absorbed and stored by organisms for the duration of their lives. When the organisms die, the exchange of carbon dioxide with the surrounding air ceases, and only decay has any effect. The half-life of C-14 is 5,730 years. Scientists claim that they can calculate the age of a fossil because they know the approximate C-14 concentration in a living being and can measure what is left thousands of years later. The further back one goes in time, the less radioactive carbon there is, and the limits of what can be measured is reached. Scientists claim that the amount of C-14 decreases rapidly after 40,000 to 50,000 years. They also admit that they can only date material that old if it is completely free of modern carbon contamination, which even in trace amounts can mask the signal. Hence, the radiocarbon clock is inaccurate. Instead of being absolute, the dates are relative and only provide age estimates.

Another problem with radiocarbon dating assumes that the C-14 formation in the upper atmosphere is constant. This is not the case. The degree varies. The only constant about the Earth's magnetic field is its variability. It becomes stronger and weaker as a result of processes deep within the Earth. However, the magnetic field protects the Earth from cosmic radiation. The stronger the magnetic field, the deeper the radiation penetrates and the more nitrogen is converted to C-14. The Earth's magnetic field must have been highly variable during the Aurignacian, the period 30,000 to 40,000 years ago when Neanderthals and modern humans are thought to have met in Europe, because radiocarbon content in the atmosphere fluctuates enormously. It is difficult to say how C-14 behaved in the atmosphere all this time.

In conclusion, all C-14 data must be interpreted. Even for the period of 5,000 to 4,000 B.C., there is no accuracy in C-14 data, and so anything beyond this time is pure guesswork.

The second method evolutionists rely on is the **fossil index system**. Evolutionists admit that no evolution is taking place in the present time and note that only "neutral drift" is taking place and observable. Yet, they interpret the fossil record as proof that evolution has occurred in pre-historic times. While radiometric dating claims to provide absolute dates (such as "30,000 to 40,000 years ago" or "150 million years plus or minus three million years"), fossil indexing provides relative dates. Simply put, relative dating states that x is older than y which is older than z. The list of index fossils follows the principle that the oldest rock formations contain simple forms of life and later formations contain more complex forms of life.

One of the early human fossils was discovered in 1891 and 1892 on the Indonesian island of Java. The fossils became known as the "Java Man." With an estimated age of 700,000 to 1,000,000 years, it was the oldest hominid fossil ever unearthed at the time of its discovery and is still considered a type specimen of the *homo erectus*. While Charles Darwin viewed the cradle of humankind in Africa, the German zoologist Ernst Haeckel was convinced that there must have been "ape-men" who lived in Lemuria, a continent located in the general area of Indonesia that allegedly disappeared over time. Eugene Dubois, a young Dutch physician, was so taken with the story that he traveled to Java to investigate. He began his excavations in an area where no prehistoric human remains were known to exist. Yet, the stratum contained the fossil bones of many distinct species of animals and five fragments of a creature that Dubois considered to be a transitional form between man and ape, a true "missing link." He named it *Anthropopithecus erectus*, the "upright chimpanzee," from *anthrōpos* ("man") and *píthēkos* ("ape" or "monkey"). Later, the Java Man was renamed *Pithecanthropus erectus*. The five fossil fragments found were a skull cap, a left thigh bone, and three teeth. They were discovered approximately 60 feet apart. Later, Dubois added a fragment of a lower jaw discovered in another part of the island but in the same geological age stratum. According to evolutionists, Dubois discoveries at the time shed significant new light on the evolutionary process of man.

However, does the principle of the fossil index system really prove evolution? The American paleontologist Carl Owen Dunbar (1891-1979) explained this principle in the following terms:

> Although the comparative study of living animals and plants may give very convincing circumstantial evidence, fossils provide the only historical, documentary evidence that life has evolved from simpler to more and more complex forms... Since fossils record life from age to age, they show the course life has taken in its gradual development. The facts that the oldest rocks bear only extinct types of relatively small and simple kinds of life, and that more and more complex types appear in successive ages, show that there has been a gradual development or unfolding of life on earth... Inasmuch as life has evolved gradually, changing from age to age, the rocks of each geologic age bear distinctive types of fossils unlike those of any other age. Conversely each kind of fossil is an index or guide fossil to some definite geologic time... Fossils thus make it possible to recognize rocks of the same age in different parts of the Earth and in this way to correlate events and work out the history of the Earth as a whole. They furnish us with a chronology on which events are arranged like pearls on a string.[40]

This is pure circular reasoning. The age of a fossil is determined by the type of rock in which it was found. The age of the rock is determined by the fossils that are found in it. The theory of evolution is the basis for dating the fossil record, which in turn is supposed to prove the theory of evolution. Worded in the most simplistic terms, the fossil records are explained by evolution, and evolution is explained by the fossil records.

---

[40] Carl Owen Dunbar, *Historical Geology* (Hoboken, NJ: John Wiley & Sons, 1960), pp. 47-48.

The German paleontologist Otto Heinrich Schindewolf (1896-1971) demonstrated this circular reasoning when he wrote:

> The only chronometric scale applicable in geologic history for the stratigraphic classification of rocks and for dating geologic events exactly is furnished by the fossils. Owing to the irreversibility of evolution, they offer an unambiguous time scale for relative age determinations and for world-wide correlations of rocks.[41]

The author and editor Robert Heron Rastall (1871-1950) admitted in the *Encyclopedia Britannica*:

> It cannot be denied that from a strictly philosophical standpoint, geologists are here arguing in a circle. The succession of organisms has been determined by the study of their remains imbedded in the rocks, and the relative ages of the rocks are determined by the remains of the organisms they contain.[42]

It needs to be noted that Rastall did not end his analysis there but stated that the circular reasoning is merely an "apparent paradox" and that the arguments for the fossil index system are "perfectly conclusive."[43]

In practice, the deposits of fossils are rarely uniform and not in the succession that would fit the evolutionary theory. This argument was brought forward by Walter E. Lammerts (1904-1996), an American author, plant researcher, horticulturist, and rose breeder. In an article published in *Christianity Today*, he wrote:

> The actual percentage of areas showing this progressive order from the simple to the complex is surprisingly small. Indeed formations with very complex forms of life are often found resting directly on the basic granites. Furthermore, I have in my own files

---

[41] Otto H. Schindewolf, "Comments on Some Stratigraphic Terms," *American Journal of Science*, Vol. 255, June 1957, p. 394.

[42] Robert H. Rastall, *Encyclopedia Britannica*, Vol. 10 (Chicago, IL: William Benton Publisher, 1956), p. 168.

[43] Ibid.

a list of over 500 cases that attest to a reverse order, that is, simple forms of life resting on top of more advanced types.[44]

An intriguing discovery was made in the four Mount Carmel caves of Tabun, Jamal, El Wad, and Skhul. The caves and their terraces can be found on the south side of the Nahal Me'arot/Wadi el-Mughara valley. This steep-sided valley that opens to the coastal plain on the west side of the Carmel range provides the background of a prehistoric habitat. The site is said to contain cultural deposits representing half a million years of human evolution from the Lower Paleolithic to the present, thus providing a definitive chronological framework at a critical period of human development. Yet, scientists discovered remains of two types of man that according to them were not contemporary: the Cro-Magnon man and the Neanderthal man.

Another discovery that disproves the fossil index method is that of dinosaur tracks. The Paluxy River basin in North Texas contains one of the heaviest concentrations of dinosaur tracks in the entire United States. Alongside those dinosaur tracks, there can also be found fossilized human footprints. The findings are admittedly highly controversial, as some of the human footprints were carved into the rock by people. However, even one such finding is sufficient to refute the whole Darwinian theory, and as of yet, the controversy is still ongoing with both sides presenting new evidence for their hypotheses. The American scientific editor and amateur astronomer Albert C. Ingalls (1888-1958) summarized the implications of these discoveries in the following way:

> If man, or even his ape ancestor, or even the ape ancestor's early mammal ancestor, existed as far back as in the carboniferous period in any shape, then the whole science of geology is so completely wrong that all geologists will resign their jobs... Hence, for the present at least, science rejects the attractive explanation that

---

[44] Walter E. Lammerts, "Growing Doubts: Is Evolutionary Theory Valid?", *Christianity Today*, Vol. VI, September 14, 1962, p. 4.

man made these mysterious prints in the mud of carboniferous period with his feet.[45]

In summary, the two sides draw their conclusions regarding the tracks based on their view of evolution. Those who accept evolution as fact will deny that man has existed in the age of the dinosaurs, while those who believe in the biblical creation account have no issue with taking the findings at face value.

Before it can be legitimately concluded that the theory of evolution is the best explanation for the fossil record, two questions must be answered:

1. Are the ages of rocks determinable independent of the theory of evolution, which is supposed to be derived from the fossil record? Thus far, the answer to this question is no.
2. Is the theory of evolution the only theory that can satisfactorily explain the fossil data? The answer to this question is no. Another explanation is the Flood.

Only if both of these questions can be answered with yes can it be said that the evolutionary theory is the best explanation for the fossil record.

Another problem evolutionists face is the missing links. There should be many such links in the evolutionary development of animals, and there should be many remains of each missing link, yet there are none. As Kerkut stated, the evolutionary theory rests on the belief that "fish, amphibia, reptiles, birds and mammals are interrelated."[46] Yet, he confessed that many key fossil transitions are not well documented, nor does science offer a satisfactory method of dating the fossils. While some of Kerkut's observations may be outdated and more recent findings suggest many transitional fossils, without a reliable method, evolutionists cannot determine which living organism came first.

---

[45] Albert G. Ingalls, "The Carboniferous Mystery," *Scientific American*, January 1940, CLXII, p. 14.

[46] Kerkut, *Implications of Evolution*, p. 153.

In conclusion, the fossil record does not show an advancement from the simple to the complex. Despite the billions of known fossils, there is an undeniable absence of transitional forms between all higher forms of life.

## 4. Conclusion

Those who express skepticism about the evolutionary theory are frequently labeled "unscientific," because the popular belief is that this theory has been proven beyond all doubt. However, after examining several fundamental flaws in this theory, we conclude that it lacks the tried scientific data to demonstrate that it is more than a working hypothesis. As a science, evolution has a long way to go, and skepticism is growing in both the general population and the scientific community. An editorial that was published in the renowned multidisciplinary science journal *Nature* in 2008 expresses the urgency for evolutionary scientists:

> Evolution is a scientific fact, and every organization whose research depends on it should explain why... Creationism is strong in the United States and, according to the Parliamentary Assembly of the Council of Europe, worryingly on the rise in Europe... But die-hard creationists aren't a sensible target for raising awareness. What matters are those citizens who aren't sure about evolution — as much as 55% of the US population according to some surveys.
>
> As the National Academy of Sciences and Padian have shown, it is possible to summarize the reasons why evolution is in effect as much a scientific fact as the existence of atoms or the orbiting of Earth round the Sun, even though there are plenty of refinements to be explored. Yet some actual and potential heads of state refuse to recognize this fact as such. And creationists have a tendency to play on the uncertainties displayed by some citizens. Evolution is of profound importance to modern biology and medicine. Accordingly, anyone who has the ability to explain the evidence behind

this fact to their students, their friends and relatives should be given the ammunition to do so. Between now and the 200th anniversary of Charles Darwin's birth on 12 February 2009, every science academy and society with a stake in the credibility of evolution should summarize evidence for it on their website and take every opportunity to promote it.[47]

In 2001, the Discovery Institute, an American public policy think tank, drafted a statement of scientific dissent from Darwinism. Over one thousand international scientists have signed this statement publicly. One of them is the American philosopher, biologist, and author David Berlinski. He states: "Darwin's theory of evolution is the great white elephant of contemporary thought. It is large, almost completely useless, and the object of superstitious awe."[48] Another signee is Michael Egnor, professor of neurosurgery and pediatrics at State University of New York:

> We know intuitively that Darwinism can accomplish some things, but not others. The question is what is that boundary? Does the information content in living things exceed that boundary? Darwinists have never faced those questions. They've never asked scientifically, can random mutation and natural selection generate the information content in living things.[49]

Marcos Eberlin, member of the Brazilian Academy of Sciences and founder of the Thomson Mass Spectrometry Laboratory, states on the same website:

> As a (bio)chemist I become [sic] most skeptical about Darwinism when I was confronted with the extreme intricacy of the genetic code and its many most intelligent strategies to code, decode and protect its information, such as the U x T and ribose x deoxyribose exchanges for the DNA/RNA pair and the translation of its 4-base language to the 20AA language of life that absolutely relies on a

---

[47] "Spread the Word," *Nature*, Vol. 451, 10 January 2008, p. 108.
[48] Retrieved from https://dissentfromdarwin.org on 17 September 2021.
[49] Retrieved from https://dissentfromdarwin.org/scientists/ on 17 September 2021.

diversity of exquisite molecular machines made by the products of such translation forming a chicken-and-egg dilemma that evolution has no chance at all to answer.[50]

The American microbiologist Ivonne Boldt summarizes the main argument in the debate well:

> When Darwinian proponents claim there is no controversy regarding the cohesiveness of the scientific evidence for evolution as creator, they are merely expressing a heartfelt desire... There is a growing contingent of scientists who have found the evidence for Darwinian evolution wanting, and who are ready and willing to debate Darwinists on scientific grounds.[51]

Finally, the American chemist and nanotechnologist James Mitchell Tour explains what a healthy scientific skepticism means practically in university settings:

> Those who think scientists understand the issues of prebiotic chemistry are wholly misinformed. Nobody understands them. Maybe one day we will. But that day is far from today. It would be far more helpful (and hopeful) to expose students to the massive gaps in our understanding. They may find a firmer—and possibly a radically different—scientific theory. The basis upon which we as scientists are relying is so shaky that we must openly state the situation for what it is: it is a mystery.[52]

The laws of thermodynamics explain the facts, but they do not explain why the world moves from order to chaos, from life to decay. The Bible provides the answer. Psalm 102:25-26 states:

> *[25]Of old did you lay the foundation of the earth; And the heavens are the work of your hands. [26]They shall perish, but you shall*

---

[50] Ibid.

[51] Ibid.

[52] James M. Tour, "Animadversions of a Synthetic Chemist," *Inference*, Chemistry/Critical Essay, Vol. 2, No. 2, May 2016.

endure; Yea, all of them shall wax old like a garment; As a vesture shalt you change them, and they shall be changed.

Romans 8:20-22 adds:

> [20]For the creation was subjected to vanity, not of its own will, but by reason of him who subjected it, in hope [21]that the creation itself also shall be delivered from the bondage of corruption into the liberty of the glory of the children of God. [22]For we know that the whole creation groans and travails in pain together until now.

These verses verify the Second Law of Thermodynamics and reiterate that there is a tendency in nature toward decay and death. This tendency was set in motion by the fall of man into sin (Gen. 3).

The biblical imperative of how to deal with the theory of evolution is provided in II Corinthians 10:3-6:

> [3]For though we walk in the flesh, we do not war according to the flesh [4](for the weapons of our warfare are not of the flesh, but mighty before God to the casting down of strongholds); [5]casting down imaginations, and every high thing that is exalted against the knowledge of God, and bringing every thought into captivity to the obedience of Messiah; [6]and being in readiness to avenge all disobedience, when your obedience shall be made full.

The theory of evolution tries to answer the question of the development of life apart from God. Believers are to battle anything that exalts itself against the knowledge of God. Consequently, the biblical imperative as provided in the above verses gives us marching orders on how to deal with such theories.

## C. Questions and Study Suggestions

**Question 1:** What is the one flaw in evolutionism that makes this doctrine wrong in your eyes?

**Question 2:** What is theistic evolution?

**Question 3:** How do creationism and evolutionism impact a person's worldview?

**Question 4:** In this chapter, we noted that the laws of thermodynamics explain the facts, but they do not explain why the world moves from order to chaos, from life to decay. The Bible provides the answer. Then Psalm 102:25-26 and Romans 8:20-22 were quoted. In your own words, how do these verses contradict the theory of evolution?

**Question 5:** In your opinion, what takes more faith: believing in evolution or believing in a God who created the heavens and the earth?

**Study Suggestion 1:** The biblical imperative of how to deal with the theory of evolution is provided in II Corinthians 10:3-6. Explain the marching orders this passage provides.

Man and Sin

**Chapter III:**

# Creationism

The term "creationism" refers to the belief that the universe, all matter, and the various forms of life originate from specific acts of divine creation rather than from natural processes such as evolution. Within the field of creationism, there are two schools of thought: young earth creationism and old earth creationism. Young earth creationists believe that God directly created the universe in six literal days and that the earth is relatively young. Old earth creationists claim that God created the universe and its inhabitants, including a literal Adam and Eve, over a much longer period of time and that the earth is about 4.5 billion years old.

## A. Scriptures and the Term *Yom*

This author holds to the literal view of creationism and believes that the present order was created in six 24-hour periods. The following Scriptures support this view: Genesis 1:1–2:3; Exodus 20:11; 31:17; Psalm 33:6, 9; Hebrews 4:4, 10.

People who want to fit Genesis 1 into evolutionary and geological theories claim that the Hebrew word for "day," *yom*, does not have to mean 24 hours but could refer to a longer period of time, even millions of years. It is true that when the word *yom* is used by itself, it could refer to a longer period of time, though no example exists in the Scriptures where it means millions of years. For example, the expression "Day of YHWH" ("Day of Jehovah" or "Day of the LORD") refers to a period of seven years. However, whenever *yom* is used with a number or numeral, it always means 24 hours. Each time *yom* is found in the creation account of Genesis 1, it is used with a numeral: day one, day two, etc. This alone shows that the days of Genesis were 24-hour days.

However, there is more. Not only is the word *yom* followed by a numeral, but it is also followed by the phrase *evening and morning*, and this phrase again limits *yom* to 24 hours.

Furthermore, the Sabbath law, as given to Israel in the Law of Moses, is based upon the six days of creation and the seventh day of rest. These laws would become meaningless if the days of creation were not 24-hour days.

Finally, in Genesis 1:14-19, the fourth day of creation is described. The verses mention "days," "years," "signs," and "seasons," showing that already within Genesis 1 there is the normal system of time in operation. These terms would also become meaningless if the days of creation were not normal 24-hour periods.

By itself, Genesis 1:1 does not speak of an old earth or a young earth. Therefore, the proof for one or the other doctrine must be based on arguments outside this verse. However, according to exegesis, the term *yom* as used in Genesis 1 cannot refer to more than 24 hours. Hence, the six days of creation were literal 24-hour days.

## B. The Creation Account of Genesis 1:1–2:3

### 1. Genesis 1:1

Genesis 1 begins with the creation of the cosmos: *In the beginning God created the heavens and the earth*. The creation of the cosmos precedes the creation work that took place in six days. The verse is an independent clause introducing the entire section.

The first three words, *In the beginning*, are an English translation of just one Hebrew word, *Bereishit*. This term simply means "in the beginning," but does not provide any information as to when this beginning was. It refers to the first phase of a step, and in Genesis 1:1, this first phase is the beginning of the universe as we now know it.

Chronologically, John 1:1 precedes Genesis 1:1. It states: *In the beginning was the Word, and the Word was with God, and the Word was God*. Then, John 1:3 notes that the universe was created through the Word, which, according to verses 14 and 17, is the Messiah. Hence, although John 1:1 begins with the same phrase, "In the beginning," chronologically speaking, the verse precedes Genesis 1:1.

The second Hebrew word in Genesis 1:1 is *bara*, which means "created." In the Hebrew language, there are certain words that are used only of God, never of man. The English language uses the word "create" with regard to both God and man, but in the Bible, this word for "create" is used only of God. The term *bara* may be used to designate creation out of nothing or creation out of something. Either way, it is still a work that only God can do. Therefore, something that has been *bara*—that has been created—is new, fresh, and good. The word *bara* also contains within it the concepts of shaping, forming, and transforming.

In the context of Genesis 1:1, *bara* means that God called the universe into existence *ex nihilo*, meaning "out of nothing." Paul confirmed this fact when he stated in Romans 4:17b: *God, who gives life to the dead, and calls the things that are not, as though they were*. Hebrews 11:3 states: *the worlds were framed by the word of God, so that what is seen has not been made of things which appear*. Here, God is viewed as the Creator of both the material and immaterial universes, and it is through His creative action that they came into existence.

There is only one word in Hebrew that is related to *bara*. This term is *briyah*, which has the same root as *bara*. This is a feminine noun that is used only in one place in the entire Hebrew Bible, namely, in Numbers 16:30a, where it also refers to God's fashioning something new: *But if Jehovah make a new thing*.

In the Hebrew Bible, *bara* is found a total of forty-eight times. In the first chapter of Genesis alone, the word is used three times in terms of God's creation: In verse 1, it is used in the context of the creation of the universe; in verse 21, it is used of living creatures; and in verse 27, it is used of man.

There are five different ways, in which *bara* is used in the Scriptures. First, the term describes God's act of creating the universe and its contents in Genesis 1:1. *Bara* is also found this way in Psalm 89:12, which explains that God created *the north and the south*; in Isaiah 40:26, where God created the *host of heavens*; in Isaiah 40:28, which describes God as *the Creator of the ends of the earth*; and in Isaiah 42:5, which states that God *created the heavens*.

A second way *bara* is used is in reference to the cosmos and the cosmic forces of nature. For example, in Isaiah 45:7, God notes that He created darkness and calamity: *I form the light, and create darkness; I make peace, and create evil; I am Jehovah, that does all these things*. According to Amos 4:13a, He also created the winds: *For, lo, he that forms the mountains, and creates the wind*.

A third way *bara* is used is with regard to living creatures. For example, in Genesis 1:21, it is used of animal life. Six verses later, in verse 27, it appears three times in reference to human life. In Genesis 5:1-2, it is again used three times of human life. It is then used of both man and animals in Genesis 6:7. In Deuteronomy 4:32, it is used of man, as well as in Psalm 89:47 and Isaiah 45:12.

The fourth way *bara* is used is in regard to Israel (Isa. 43:1, 15; Mal. 2:10) and the believing remnant (Eccl. 12:1; Isa. 43:7).

The fifth way the word is used concerns the transformation or renewal of things. This usage is found in Numbers 16:30, where God creates *a new thing* in the earth; in Psalm 51:10, where God creates *a clean heart*; in Isaiah 41:20, where God creates the waters in the desert; in Isaiah 45:8, where God creates *salvation*; in Isaiah 57:19, where God creates *peace*; in Isaiah 65:17, where God creates a renewal of *the heavens and the earth* for the Messianic kingdom; in Isaiah 65:18, where God creates a new *Jerusalem*; and in Jeremiah 31:22, where God creates *a new thing*, namely, a woman who *shall encompass a man*.

The next key word in Genesis 1:1 is *Elohim*, the Hebrew term for "God," which shows that the Creator is the beginning of all things. God existed before all things. There is no attempt in Genesis to prove His existence because it is assumed to be true. From a biblical perspective, only a fool says that there is no God (Ps. 14:1).

*Elohim* is a plural Hebrew word. It would be wrong to say that this term proves the Trinity, but it does open the door for the concept of a plurality in the Godhead. The point of the word is that God is self-sufficient; there is no need of anyone or anything else. God is eternal and unchangeable.

Literally, Genesis 1:1 reads "In the beginning God," and this phrase is the foundation of all theology. God is self-existent. He is unknowable except when He reveals Himself. He is answerable to no one.

The next phrase to consider in the discussion of Genesis 1:1 is "the heavens and the earth." The heavens and the earth are two separate entities, as Psalm 115:16 shows: *The heavens are the heavens of Jehovah; But the earth hath he given to the children of men*. The term "heavens" includes everything that constitutes the parts of the universe. It is plural because it includes the first heaven, which is the atmosphere, and the second heaven, which is outer space. The creation account of Genesis 1 shows that matter is not eternal but had a definite beginning with God. The term "earth" refers to that which becomes the center of God's program. Psalm 8 emphasizes that God's program concerns man, who is found only on this planet.

## 2. Genesis 1:2

Genesis 1:2 states: *And the earth was waste and void; and darkness was upon the face of the deep: and the Spirit of God moved upon the face of the waters*. In Hebrew, this verse begins with the phrase *vehaaretz*, meaning "and the earth." This shows that the earth is now the focus, not the universe. When the subject comes before the predicate, the emphasis is on the subject, stating something new about the subject. It describes the circumstances of the world prior to Genesis 1:3, but not necessarily as a result of verse 1.

In the Masoretic Text, the verse begins with a *vav* disjunctive, meaning "now," rather than a *vav* conjunctive, meaning "and." This shows that the verse is not sequential, but means "and then." It shows that verse 2 is not the result of verse 1, nor is it a development of verse 1. The disjunctive argues against the chaos described in verse 2 as being some kind of an intermediate state in God's work at the time of creation. Isaiah 45:18 makes that same point: *For thus says Jehovah that created the heavens, the God that formed the earth and made it, that established it and created it not a waste, that formed it to be inhabited: I am Jehovah; and there is none else*. God did not create the world *a waste*. Hence, what Genesis 1:2 is describing is the state of the world prior to the first day of creation, which begins with verse 3.

Scholars have generally chosen to resolve this "disjunctive predicament" here in two ways. The first way is called "the initial chaos view." This view teaches that verse 1 gives the general account and summary of the whole chapter. Verse 2 follows by giving a description of the chaos at the beginning of creation. Then, verse 3 relates the beginning of God's work of creation. In this view, the original creation is not itself in the account, but only a recreation of it.

The second way to solve the disjunctive predicament is called "the gap theory." Due to the false teaching of evolution, this expression has received a backlash. However, if one considers the actual meaning of the term, it shows that the criticism is without merit. The gap theory teaches that in Genesis 1:1, there was an original creation in a perfect state. Then the fall of Satan, described in Ezekiel 28:11-19, occurred. The fall of Satan resulted in divine judgment, which, in turn, led to the chaos of verse 2. Hence, the gap theory views verse 1 as the original creation, before the fall of Satan caused it to become a chaos, and views verse 2 as describing the chaos that resulted from divine judgment.

The gap of time between verses 1 and 2 need not be very long at all. Also, it may not be used as a convenient place to fit in such things as the geological ages, the fossil record, and the dinosaurs. Before the fall of Adam, there was no death. Hence, the extinction of the dinosaurs occurred after Adam fell into sin. The gap is there for only one reason: the fall of Satan. This event accounts for the chaos described in verse 2.

The Hebrew term for "was" in Genesis 1:2 is *hayetah*. This is the third person feminine singular perfect tense of the Hebrew root *hayah*, and the primary meaning is "was." Here, though, it is better taken in its secondary meaning of "became." Normally, the term requires a different kind of construction to mean "became." However, in other places, even within the book of Genesis, we see that the word means "became" when used in the same kind of construction as here in verse 2a. For example, in Genesis 3:20, Eve became *the mother of all living*; in Genesis 3:22, *man is become as one of us*; in Genesis 21:20, Ishmael *became, as he grew up, an archer*; and in Genesis 37:20, the question is asked, *what will become of* [Joseph's] *dream?* Hence, according to Genesis 1:2, the earth became desolate and waste. Again, this interpretation harmonizes very well with Isaiah 45:18, which states that God did not create the earth waste and void. In other words, He did not create the earth in the form in which it is found in Genesis 1:2.

These two words, *waste* and *void*, are a translation of the Hebrew terms *tohu va-vohu*, with *va* meaning "and." The phrase *tohu va-vohu* is used twice elsewhere. In the two other places where the words are used together, they very clearly refer to divine judgment. For example, Isaiah 34:11 teaches that God caused *confusion* and *emptiness*; and in Jeremiah 4:23, the phrase "waste and void" is viewed as the antithesis to the Genesis creation account.

The Hebrew term *vohu* is found only in these three passages, and always in connection with *tohu*, which is used by itself seventeen times in the Hebrew Bible. *Tohu* does not always carry the connotation of divine judgment, but it is always something that is quite negative. In the ASV of 1901, it is translated in the following ways: in Deuteronomy 32:10, as *desert land*; twice in I Samuel 12:21, as *vain*; in Job

6:18, as *waste* or "nothing"; in Job 12:24, as *wilderness*; in Job 26:7, as *empty space*; in Psalm 107:40, as *waste*; in Isaiah 24:10, as *the waste city*; in Isaiah 29:21, as *a thing of nought*; in Isaiah 40:17, as *nothing*; in Isaiah 40:23, as *nothing*; in Isaiah 41:29, as *confusion*; in Isaiah 44:9, as *vanity*; in Isaiah 45:18, as *waste*; in Isaiah 45:19 and 49:4, as *vain*; and in Isaiah 59:4, as *vanity*.

Another point to note regarding *tohu va-vohu* is that there are two examples of syntagms in Genesis 1:1-2. (Syntagms are words that occur together to denote one unique concept.) The first example is "heaven and earth," a phrase that refers to the totality of the ordered universe. The second example is *tohu va-vohu*, "waste and void," referring to the totality of judgment and chaos.

In summary, the phrase *tohu va-vohu* carries the meaning of chaos and desolation. The conclusion is that verses 1-2 describe an orderly world and a disorderly chaos. Of course, these cannot apply to the same thing at the same time. In other words, verses 1 and 2 cannot be contemporary, but must be chronological in sequence. In Genesis 1:1, the earth and the heavens are created in perfect order. Then, sometime later, this chaos—the chaos of unformed matter which caused it to become undifferentiated, unorganized, confused, and lifeless—came as a result of Satan's fall. Thus, the earth "became" formless and empty.

The next phrase to consider in Genesis 1:2 is: *and darkness was upon the face of the deep*. There are two key terms in this phrase, the first of which is "darkness." Throughout Scripture, this term represents evil and death and something that is not conducive to life. It is also a common symbol of divine judgment (e.g. Ex. 10:15, 21-23; I Sam. 2:9; Job 3:4-5; Ps. 35:6; 105:28; Isa. 8:22; 13:10; 45:7; Joel 2:2; Eph. 6:12). Hence, both the chaos and the darkness are the result of Satan's fall. The second key term is "the deep," or *tehom* in Hebrew. The basic meanings of *tehom* include "the salty deep," "the primeval ocean," and "the abyss." Psalm 104:6 states that God covered the earth with *the deep* as a garment. Proverbs 8:24 states that God's wisdom existed before there were any *depths*. Isaiah 51:10 refers to *the waters of the great deep*. In Genesis, the primeval world ocean or *the deep* was without personality and without any autonomy of its own.

Verse 2 describes the result of judgment, which was the fall of Satan as described in Ezekiel 28:11-19. This Ezekiel passage teaches that the earth, as created by God in Genesis 1:1, served as the second of Satan's six abodes.[53] When God judged Satan, He also judged everything under Satan's authority, including the earth. The original planet Earth was a beautiful mineral garden that exuded light from a variety of precious stones. As a result of Satan's fall, the earth became formless and empty. It was totally covered by salt water, with the precious stones and dry land no longer visible. The stones of fire no longer exuded light. Instead, there was now darkness *upon the face of the deep*. This means that saltwater was one of the results of Satan's fall, and it helps to explain why, when God creates the new heavens and the new earth in Revelation 21–22, there will be no oceans or no seas. This new creation will be a return to the original state of the earth. After the present system ends, the new earth will look the way it did before Satan's fall.

The next phrase to consider in Genesis 1:2 is: *and the Spirit of God moved upon the face of the waters*. This is the first introduction to the Third Person of the Trinity, the Spirit of God. According to John 1:1-3, the agent of creation was God the Son, and the means was the *Ruach HaKodesh*, God the Holy Spirit. The Spirit introduced the work of the Son by moving *upon the face of the waters*. The Hebrew word for "moved" is *merachephet*, which means "to hover," "to brood," "to flutter," "to shake," or "to fly." In Deuteronomy 32:11, *merachephet* is used of an eagle hovering over her young, thus caring for and protecting the chicks. The Spirit's hovering means that He was keeping the formless, foreboding darkness in check and was preparing the

---

[53] For more details on the six abodes of Satan, see: Arnold G. Fruchtenbaum, *A Study of the Angelic Realm: Angelology, Satanology, and Demonology* (San Antonio, TX: Ariel Ministries, 2020); Arnold G. Fruchtenbaum, *The Footsteps of the Messiah: A Study of the Sequence of Prophetic Events* (San Antonio, TX: Ariel Ministries, 2021), pp. 525-543.

earth for creation. Hence, like the Father and the Son, this Third Person of the Trinity was actively involved in the work of creation (cf. Job 26:13).

## 3. Genesis 1:3-31

Since this is a book on anthropology, the account of the six days of creation will focus primarily on the creation of man. For a detailed study of the rest of the verses, see the author's commentary on Genesis.

There is a basic symmetry throughout Genesis 1:3-31, with every single day of the six days beginning the same way: *And God said*. All things came into being at God's Word, something also emphasized by Psalm 33:6-9. "And God said" is an introductory, creative clause, and it is the first of seven specific steps. The second step is the fiat: *Let there be*. The third step is the fulfillment: *and there was* or *and it was so*. The fourth step contains the description of the action: *And God made*. The fifth step is the act of naming or blessing something: either *And God called* or *And God blessed*. The sixth step is God's evaluation, an expression of divine satisfaction: *and God saw that it was good*. The seventh and final step is the terminus: *And there was evening and there was morning*, followed by the number of the *day*. These, then, are the seven specific steps in each of the first six days, a period of time that rectifies the problem of the formlessness and emptiness in verse 2.

Again, one Hebrew word, *tohu*, emphasized the concept of the earth being without form. This formlessness is remedied by the first three days of creation. During these days, three elements were divided from one another: first, light was separated from darkness on the first day; second, the air or sky was separated from the water or sea on the second day; and third, the land was separated from the plants on the third day.

The second Hebrew word was *vohu*, which emphasized the concept of emptiness. The problem of the earth's emptiness was rectified on the second three days of creation when "decoration" was provided: On the fourth day, the lights were placed into the firmament for the day and night; on the fifth day, fowl was put in the air and fish into the sea; on the sixth day, animals and man were created for the dry land and plants.

In this manner, the problems of the earth's formlessness and emptiness described in verse 2 are now solved.

## 4. The Sixth Day of Creation: Genesis 1:24-27

On the crucial sixth day of creation, God accomplished two major works: the creation of animal life (vv. 24-25) and the creation of the human race (vv. 26-27). Verse 24 introduces God's creative work on that day: *And God said, Let the earth bring forth living creatures after their kind, cattle, and creeping things, and beasts of the earth after their kind: and it was so.* According to Genesis 2:19, animals were created out of the ground. God created three categories of land animals, the first of which was *cattle*. This English term is the translation of the Hebrew word *behemah*, which does not only refer to cows but to all sorts of domesticated animals. The second category is *creeping things*, both large and small. The Hebrew term is *remes* and refers to creatures that have either no legs or very short legs, so that they appear to move on their bellies. This applies to both reptiles and amphibians. The third category is *the beasts of the earth*, which refers to the wild animals that simply cannot be domesticated.

The results of God's creative work are seen in verse 25: *And God made the beasts of the earth after their kind, and the cattle after their kind, and everything that creeps upon the ground after its kind: and God saw that it was good.* The result of God's creative work on that day was that there were now wild and domesticated animals and creatures such as reptiles and amphibians. The phrase "God saw that it was good" concludes the passage.

An important observation is that both higher animals and man were created on the same day. This truth helps to explain the fact that man is similar to higher animals both in his physical makeup and genetically. Animals and man were created on the same day to live on the same part of the earth, the dry land, so there are these similarities. The difference between man and animals in this category lies in the spiritual nature of God-likeness. Only man has the conscious ability to truly know God.

Verse 26a introduces the creation of man: *And God said, Let us make man in our image, after our likeness*. Again, the creative work begins with the customary "And God said." But in this case, these words do not introduce a new day, but a new work. What was about to be created was unique. Man was to be the high point and final stage of creation.

There is now also a change to the fiat: Let us make. Up to this point, God had been using the jussive form, meaning "let there be." Now there is a switch from the jussive to the cohortative form of "Let us make," which shows this to be a unique, momentous event, a different kind of creation. God referred to Himself using the plural pronouns "us" and "our." This does not prove the Trinity as such, but it does open the door to the concept of plurality in the Godhead and is the first of several such instances. The personal pronouns could not, as some people teach, refer to angels because, as far as the work of creation is concerned, God alone did this work. There are no angels mentioned anywhere in this context. Furthermore, the expression "Let us make" does not refer to a consultation. If God were consulting with an assembly of angels, the text would have told us that, just as it does in I Kings 22:19-23, when He consulted with the angelic court.

The Hebrew word for "man" is *adam*. This is a general term meaning "mankind," including both males and females.

The Hebrew term for "in our image" is *tzelem*. This word can refer either to an original image or to an imitation and can be used both in a good sense and in a bad one. In a good sense, it appears as it does here, where man is created in the image of God. In a bad sense, it is used to refer to idols or imitations in such passages as Numbers 33:52; I Samuel 6:5, 11; II Kings 11:18; II Chronicles 23:17; Ezekiel 7:20; 16:17;

23:14; and Amos 5:26. It is also used for less concrete elements. For example, in Psalm 39:6, the word *tzelem* is used of a phantom in parallel with vanity; and in Psalm 73:20, it is paralleled with a dream, also a sense of unreality. What exactly it means that man was created in the image of God will be discussed in the next chapter.

Man was created both in the image of God and also in His likeness. The Hebrew term for "likeness" is *demut*, meaning "model" or "copy." This is used exclusively as the preferred word in describing a theophany, a visible manifestation of God's presence. The word is used this way a number of times in the first ten chapters of Ezekiel. The fact that man was made in the likeness of God emphasizes his uniqueness. Man was created uniquely different than the animal kingdom, a quality also emphasized by Psalm 8:3-5.

Genesis 1:26b shows the purpose of the creation of man: *and let them have dominion over the fish of the sea, and over the birds of the heavens, and over the cattle, and over all the earth, and over every creeping thing that creeps upon the earth*. The purpose of man's creation was that he would have dominion over the earth. Having dominion was a consequence of having been created in the image of God, but it was not the content of the image. God has dominion over all of creation, and since man was created in God's image, he was now given dominion over the earth. Man thus replaced Satan as the authority over the earth (Gen. 1:1; Ps. 8:6-8; Ezek. 28:11-19; Heb. 2:5-9). When Satan fell, God judged him and the earth, resulting in the chaos of Genesis 1:2 and Satan's loss of his dominion.

The passage then specifies the particular areas over which man is to exercise dominion: first, *the fish of the sea*, meaning the sea life; second, *the birds of the heavens*, meaning the bird life; third, *the cattle*, meaning domesticated animals; fourth, *all the earth*, meaning the physical earth; and fifth, *every creeping thing that creeps upon the earth*, meaning amphibians and reptiles.

Verse 27 next shows the fulfillment of God's creative work: *And God created man in his own image, in the image of God created he him; male and female created he them*. In Hebrew, the verb *bara* is used three times in this verse to show that a high point is reached. First, it is used of man's creation. Second, it is also used of the creation of the divine image. Third, it is used to emphasize the creation of the two sexes, both on the sixth day. Man was not divided into species, not after their kind, because both male and female have the image of God. Man was the final act of creation.

Theologians point out that when man was created, he was *posse non peccare*, which is a Latin expression meaning "able not to sin." But man was also *posse peccare*, meaning "able to sin." This was man's status before the fall. After the fall, man became *non posse non peccare*, "not able not to sin." In other words, he could not help but sin.

The rest of the creation account is concerned with the establishment of the Edenic Covenant in verses 28-30 and a conclusion in verse 31.[54]

One final note about this sixth day of creation concerns men and women. Both were created on the same day as the crowning elements of creation. Genesis 1 does not deal with the order of the creation of male and female, but the emphasis is that God created humanity, both male and female, on the same day. Furthermore, both have the image of God, and both were given the mandate of authority over the planet in the Edenic Covenant. To be sure, there was headship, but both Adam and Eve were given the mandate of authority over the planet Earth under the Edenic Covenant.

## 5. The Theological Implications

There are four theological implications of the six days of creation in the overall context of Genesis. First, the God who created Israel is also the God who created the universe.

Second, there is an emphasis on the sovereignty of the God of creation. Everything that exists must be under God's control. Sometimes things happen because of His directive will. Events occur because God decreed them to occur, such as the flood and the events surrounding

---

[54] For information regarding the covenants, see Volume 1 of this series.

Sodom and Gomorrah. But sometimes things happen because of God's permissive will. For example, He did not direct Adam and Eve to sin, but He did permit them to sin. Either way, everything is under the sovereignty of the God of creation.

A third theological implication is the foundation of law, because the earth was created by means of the Word of God. God was before all things, and He caused all things to come into being. So there was, and is, simply no other god to obey. The God of creation laid down specific provisions, such as the Edenic Covenant. As Genesis and subsequent history continue, there will be more provisions made, such as the Law of Moses. The point is that God is the Creator, and His creation serves as the foundation for law. The same way that God creates (by means of His Word) is also the way by which He communicates His will and by which He spells out human obligations to Him.

A fourth theological implication is God's redemptive work. At the time described in Genesis 1, there was no sin. Hence, there are no clear statements about redemption, but there are some implications of the work of redemption. This is seen in two ways. First, there is the concept of going from darkness to light. While these terms are used in their physical senses, they also have spiritual implications. For example, Yeshua is called the *light of the world* (Jn. 8:12), and believers are transferred to the kingdom of the light of the Son of God. On the other hand, Satan is the prince of this darkness (e.g., Eph. 2:2). Sin is compared to darkness (e.g., Mt. 6:23; Rom. 1:21). Just as the physical creation moved from darkness to light, even so in the redemptive work of God, believers have moved from the darkness of sin to the light of salvation. A second way this redemptive work is seen is through the movement from chaos to order. Chaos is the result of sin, of Satan's fall; darkness was upon the face of the deep, and Satan is the angel of this darkness. He likes to fashion himself as a counterfeit angel of light, but in reality, he is the angel of this darkness. Sin brings chaos into the lives of unbelievers and believers as well. God has provided movement from chaos to order. For the unbeliever, he moves from chaos to order when he accepts Yeshua as his Savior. When a believer sins, he can also move from chaos to order by confessing his sin before the Lord, repenting from it, and reestablishing fellowship with God (I Jn. 1:9).

## 6. The Completion of the Creative Work: Genesis 2:1-3

The completion of God's creative work is seen in Genesis 2:1-3:

> $^1$*And the heavens and the earth were finished, and all the host of them. $^2$And on the seventh day God finished his work which he had made; and he rested on the seventh day from all his work which he had made. $^3$And God blessed the seventh day, and hallowed it; because that in it he rested from all his work which God had created and made.*

In the context of the discussion of creationism and the origin of man, the importance of this passage lies in the fact that it describes the cessation of creation. God had completed His creative work, and the function was no longer creation, but procreation.

## C. Questions and Study Suggestions

***Study Suggestion 1:*** According to the Bible, the present order was created. List the verses that support this view:

1. _____
2. _____
3. _____
4. _____
5. _____

***Study Suggestion 2:*** Explain the author's statement: "Just as the physical creation moved from darkness to light, even so in the redemptive work of God, believers have moved from the darkness of sin to the light of salvation."

***Study Suggestion 3:*** The author explains that there was a gap of time between Genesis 1:1 and 1:2. He provides several reasons for this view. How does his position differ from what is commonly referred to as the "gap theory"? Using the Hebrew terms discussed in this chapter, explain the author's view in your own words.

***Question 1:*** What does the Hebrew word *yom* mean? How does it relate to the creation account in Genesis 1:1–2:3?

***Question 2:*** In the context of the discussion of creationism and the origin of man, what is the importance of Genesis 2:1-3?

## Chapter IV:
# The Image of God in Man

According to Genesis 1:26, man was created in the image and likeness of God. What is this image of God? Does it pertain to some outward elements of man, or does it refer to inward characteristics and aspects?

## A. Introduction

According to the Bible, man is dichotomous, meaning he is made of two parts: the body (the material part) and the spirit (the immaterial part). This is brought out in Genesis 2:7: *And Jehovah God formed man of the dust of the ground, and breathed into his nostrils the breath of life; and man became a living soul.* This verse will be discussed in detail under "The Composition of Man." Of importance here is that the material part of man was formed from pre-existing matter. In the case of the first male, this pre-existing matter was *the dust of the ground.* In the case of the first woman, it was a rib, or more precisely, Adam's side (Gen. 2:21-22). In both cases, the creation happened through the immediate intervention of God. God formed Adam and Eve.

As for the immaterial part of man, God breathed into man's nostrils and made him a living soul. Hence, the soul is derived from God.

In the context of creationism, one cannot remove Adam from the picture without doing much violence to Scripture and theology. Adam was a personal, individual being. He was the first man. Other passages that bring out this fact are Genesis 1:26—5:4; I Chronicles 1:1; Job 31:33; Hosea 6:7; Matthew 19:4-5; Mark 10:7-8; Luke 3:38; Romans

5:12-19; I Corinthians 11:3-12; 15:21-22, 45; I Timothy 2:13; and Jude 14.

All human beings descend from Adam. After the flood, all nations came from Noah (Gen. 10:32). It must be noted that the Bible neither teaches the concept of race nor does the word "race" appear in Scripture. There is only one race, the human race. However, the Bible allows for divergence within species, and this concept can be seen in the Table of the Nations of Genesis 10:32.

Like all other species, from the very beginning, man could only reproduce after his own kind (Gen. 1:24), meaning a human being could never produce a monkey or vice versa. However, the created kinds of living organisms (plants, animals, and human beings) were able to produce a wide variety of subtypes or subspecies within a short period of time. Science shows that any observed change in living organisms is minor and horizontal in nature, with no net increase in genetic information leading to large, vertical change (macroevolution). When scientists find "new" species, many of these findings can be placed within the created kinds that God described in Genesis 1. Therefore, when "new" species are discovered, they simply represent the product of the diversification of the various kinds that survived the global flood. Creatures can and do diversify, or "speciate," within their own kind, and they pass on genetic material in a reshuffled way. God designed them to do so. However, they never evolve into fundamentally new creatures, as evolutionists claim. Scientists cannot observe fish evolving into other species such as birds, nor do they see any evidence of such a transition into another type of creature in the fossil record.

According to the biblical account, man is roughly 6,000 years old. Some try to argue that there are gaps in the genealogies of the Bible. However, these gaps cannot be superimposed on the Genesis genealogy. The wording of Genesis 5 and 11 does not allow for gaps.

Death entered the world with Adam, and before the fall of man in Genesis 3:1-8, there was no death. The Bible does not allow for death before Adam. Hence, all life was contemporary with Adam, including species that are extinct.

The creation account does not state how old Adam and Eve looked on the day of creation, but they were not created as infants; they were created as adults. By its very nature, creation carries with it the appearance of age. On the seventh day, Adam and Eve were one day old, but they looked like adults. They were created as adults capable of sexual intercourse.

The concept of age is important because any system of dating is dependent on the interpretation of age. From a biblical perspective, any geological system of dating must take into account the worldwide flood in order to be accurate. This flood accounts for the disappearance of groups within species, and it accounts for the fossil record.

## B. Scriptures

There are five Scripture passages that mention the image of God, and what the Bible teaches about the image of God must be deduced from these five passages.

The first passage is Genesis 1:26-27, which states:

*²⁶And God said, Let us make man in our image, after our likeness: and let them have dominion over the fish of the sea, and over the birds of the heavens, and over the cattle, and over all the earth, and over every creeping thing that creeps upon the earth. ²⁷And God created man in his own image, in the image of God created he him; male and female created he them.*

The second passage is Genesis 5:1-2:

*¹This is the book of the generations of Adam. In the day that God created man, in the likeness of God made he him; ²male and female created he them, and blessed them, and called their name Adam, in the day when they were created.*

Third comes Genesis 9:6: *Whoso sheds man's blood, by man shall his blood be shed: for in the image of God made he man.*

The fourth passage is I Corinthians 11:7: *For a man indeed ought not to have his head veiled, forasmuch as he is the image and glory of God: but the woman is the glory of the man.*

The fifth and final passage is James 3:9: *Therewith bless we the Lord and Father; and therewith curse we men, who are made after the likeness of God.*

These five passages use two different terms that need to be considered: *image* and *likeness*. As point out in a previous chapter, the Hebrew term for "image" is *tzelem*, which is used to describe three things: images that were cut out of some material, such as wood (e.g., I Sam. 6:5); a likeness and resemblance (e.g., Gen. 1:26-27; 9:6); and figuratively, mere, empty images or semblances (e.g., Dan. 2:31).

The Hebrew term for "likeness" is *demut*, which refers to similitude of external appearance and means "resemblance," "a model," or "a copy." Ezekiel used this term to describe theophanies (e.g., Ezek. 1:5, 13; 8:2; 10:21).

In the above passages, the terms "image" and "likeness" are used interchangeably. This can be seen in the fact that Genesis 1:26 used both terms, while in all others passages, either one or the other appears (Gen. 1:27 – image; Gen. 5:1 – likeness; Gen. 9:6 – image; I Cor. 11:7 – image; Jam. 3:9 – likeness). One does not have to make a sharp distinction between the two terms because the Scriptures use them interchangeably and they therefore basically mean the same thing.

## C. A Preliminary Definition of the Image of God

There are certain features, characteristics, and attributes of God that are also true of man. These features comprise the image of God in man. For example, God's likeness is seen in man's ability to rule over creation, to relate to God and other human beings, and to make use of intelligence and creativity. The most striking example, however, is that the original state of man following creation was characterized by holiness. Adam's holiness enabled him to have a face-to-face relationship with God. Yet, his holiness was not identical to God's because it was limited by the fact that Adam was a created being. Theologically, Adam's holiness is called "unconfirmed creaturely holiness." This means that his holiness was unconfirmed until he could successfully pass the tests placed before him by God. When Adam was tested, he failed, so his holiness was not confirmed; instead, he became corrupt. But the original state of the image of God in man was unconfirmed creaturely holiness, and this aspect of the image of God in man was lost in the fall and no longer exists.

Other aspects of the image of God are still there, although marred. The fact that these aspects are still present is seen in the use of the present tense in passages such as Genesis 9:6, which states: *Whoso sheds man's blood, by man shall his blood be shed: for in the image of God made he man*. The same can be seen in I Corinthians 11:7: *For a man indeed ought not to have his head veiled, forasmuch as he is the image and glory of God: but the woman is the glory of the man*. James 3:9 is another example: *Therewith bless we the Lord and Father; and therewith curse we men, who are made after the likeness of God*. Hence, while on one hand, man does not have the original state of unconfirmed creaturely holiness, there are other features of God that he still has. These other features have been marred by the fall and are no longer perfect or holy. But they are still very much there.

The fact that the image of God is still in man is the basis for respecting all humanity. This can be seen in the same three passages that were just quoted. Genesis 9:6 forbids the act of murder on the basis that the murder victim was created in the image of God. In I Corinthians 11:7, the image of God is the basis for church decorum in that men are to have their heads uncovered in the meeting of the church, while women are to cover their heads. Finally, James 3:9 forbids cursing people because the person being cursed still has the image of God in him. Hence, the image of God in man is the basis for respecting humanity.

In summary, when dealing with a working definition of the image of God in man, four points should be noted. First, the expression "image of God" refers to those features of God that are also true of man.

Second, there is one feature that no longer exists, namely, unconfirmed creaturely holiness, which was lost in the fall. Third, there are still other features that God and man share, so man still has the image of God in him, although it is marred. Fourth, even though the image of God in man is marred, enough of it still remains so that all human beings are commanded to respect others.

## D. The Components of the Image of God in Man

Six components of the image of God in man may be listed. The first component reveals what this image is not, and the other five components reveal what it is.

First, the image of God in man is not a physical likeness. The fact that man was created in the image of God does not mean that God has physical features, although God has, at times, taken on the form and appearance of a man, but this is not His regular, natural form. John 4:24 makes clear that *God is a Spirit*. Furthermore, I Timothy 1:17 and 6:16 show that God is invisible. Since God is a Spirit and invisible, He does not share the particular physical likeness and form of man.

Second, the image of God in man is a personal likeness (Gen. 2:19-20, 23). Just as God is a personality, man is a personality. Personality is defined by three attributes: intellect, emotion, and will. Whoever and whatever has these three attributes is a personality. God has intellect, emotion, and will; man has intellect, emotion, and will. This is one component of the image of God in man.

Third, the image of God in man is a spiritual likeness in that man himself has an eternal spirit within him (I Cor. 15:45). While the physical part of man can die, his immaterial part can never die. This spiritual likeness is a component of the image of God in man.

Fourth, the image of God in man is a moral likeness (Eph. 4:22-24; Col. 3:9-10). God is a moral being, and man also has a sense of morality. Even in the darkest areas of the world, there is still a sense of morality, a sense of right and wrong. This moral likeness is a component of the image of God in man.

Fifth, the image of God in man is a social likeness. God is a social being. He has always existed as a Triune God. Therefore, there has always been a continuous social interaction, a continuous social fellowship, and a continuous communication between the three Persons of the Trinity. Man shares this particular likeness with God (I Jn. 1:3). People are social beings who like to communicate and share with other people. Because of this social likeness, the believer can have fellowship with God and fellowship with other believers. This social likeness is a component of the image of God in man.

Sixth, the image of God in man is an authoritative likeness. God is sovereign. He is the sole authority over the entire universe and the only One who controls it. When God gave man authority over the animal kingdom (Gen. 1:28) and over the material universe (Gen. 9:2), He was willing to share His authority with man. Therefore, man has an authoritative likeness.

In summary, the image of God in man is not a physical likeness, but a personal, spiritual, moral, social, and authoritative likeness.

# E. The Correlation Between the Image of God and Redemption

The correlation between the image of God in man and the issue of redemption is seen in three passages, the first of which is Romans 8:29: *For whom he foreknew, he also foreordained to be conformed to the image of his Son, that he might be the firstborn among many brethren*. God had a special plan for those whom He foreknew. He foreordained them to achieve the goal of being conformed to His Son's image. The image of God in man that was marred by the fall will some day be totally restored to its pure holiness. One of the purposes of the Holy Spirit's work in the area of sanctification is to conform the believer more and more to the image of the Son of God. Once conformed, the image, now marred, will attain confirmed creaturely holiness. As a result, the Son will be *the firstborn among many brethren*, the first of many who will be like Him.

The second passage that connects the image of God with redemption is found in I Corinthians 15:49: *And as we have borne the image of the earthy, we shall also bear the image of the heavenly*. The term "heavenly" refers to God the Son. Believers are destined to bear His image. They are foreordained to be conformed more and more to this image of the Son of God. Upon arrival in heaven, they will attain the perfection of the image of the Heavenly One and will be completely conformed to it.

The third passage that connects the image of God with redemption is II Corinthians 3:18: *But we all, with unveiled face beholding as in a mirror the glory of the Lord, are transformed into the same image from glory to glory, even as from the Lord the Spirit*. Once the process of sanctification is completed, either at the rapture or upon death, believers will be thoroughly conformed to the image of God's Son. They are going to bear His image from then on and, as a result, will be changed or transformed into that same image *from glory to glory*. It is in this image that believers will reflect the *Shechinah* glory of God, meaning the visible manifestation of God's presence.

# F. Questions and Study Suggestions

**Question 1:** What is the difference between "image" and "likeness"?

**Question 2:** What does the phrase "unconfirmed creaturely holiness" mean?

**Question 3:** Is man still in the state of unconfirmed creaturely holiness?

**Study Suggestion 1:** List the three verses that show that the image of God in man is marred.
   1. _____
   2. _____
   3. _____

**Study Suggestion 2:** Although the image of God in man is marred, it is still the basis for _____ (Gen. 9:6), for _____ (I Cor. 11:7), and for _____ (Jas. 3:9).

**Study Suggestion 3:** The image of God in man is not a _____ likeness but a

_____,
_____,
_____,
_____,
and _____ likeness.

**Study Suggestion 4:** Explain the correlation between the image of God in man and redemption.

Man and Sin

# Chapter V:
# The Composition of Man

The composition of man will be studied in three sections that deal with the material part of man, the immaterial part of man, and the relationship of the material to the immaterial.

## A. The Material Part of Man

Genesis 2:7 states: *And Jehovah God formed man of the dust of the ground, and breathed into his nostrils the breath of life; and man became a living soul.* In the creation account of Genesis 1:26-27, the Hebrew word for "create" is *bara*. This term emphasizes that the creation of man was a work that only God could do. In Genesis 2:7, the term *yatzar* is used, meaning "to mold" or "to shape by design." Elsewhere in the Bible, *yatzar* is used of a potter shaping pottery (Isa. 29:16, Jer. 18:1-17); of goldsmiths who make idols (Isa. 44:9, Hab. 2:18); of the shaping of the Messiah's body in the womb (Isa. 49:5); and of things that God fashions, such as the hearts (Ps. 33:15), ears (Ps. 94:9), and eyes (Ps. 94:9). Hence, according to Genesis 2:7, God formed man just as a potter shapes a piece of clay into a bowl or a vase. The verse focuses on the material God used for this purpose: *the dust of the ground*. Although God used an already existing material to create Adam, the act of *yatzar* was still something only He could do.

The Hebrew term for "dust" is *aphar*, and the term for "ground" is *adamah*. In combination, the phrase has the connotation of dust and clay. God created man out of dust and clay, emphasizing man as ground. Another thing to note in Genesis 2:7 is the Hebrew word for "man," *adam*, which is very similar to *adamah*, the word for "dust."

Both *adam* and *adamah* come from the same Hebrew root. There is a Hebrew word play here, and one way to bring it out is to translate the phrase as God forming the "earthling" from the "earth."

The correlation of clay and dust is also found in Job 4:19, where humanity is described as dwelling *in houses of clay, whose foundation is in the dust*. Job 10:8-9 notes that God's hands formed man out of clay and can return him to dust. According to Job 33:6, man was formed out of clay, a statement that is also made in Isaiah 45:9. All of these passages emphasize the humble origins of man. Man was created out of mere earth.

As biblical theology develops this topic, this emphasis on man being formed of dust, or the ground, points out three things. First, the fact that man was created out of the ground is a symbol of man's little worth, as the following verses show:

- Genesis 18:27: *And Abraham answered and said, Behold now, I have taken upon me to speak unto the Lord, who am but dust and ashes.*
- Joshua 7:6: *And Joshua rent his clothes, and fell to the earth upon his face before the ark of Jehovah until the evening, he and the elders of Israel; and they put dust upon their heads.*
- I Samuel 2:8a: *He raises up the poor out of the dust.*
- I Kings 16:2a: *Forasmuch as I exalted thee out of the dust.*
- II Kings 13:7b: *for the king of Syria destroyed them, and made them like the dust in threshing.*
- Job 2:12b: *and they rent every one his robe, and sprinkled dust upon their heads toward heaven.*
- Psalm 18:42: *Then did I beat them small as the dust before the wind; I did cast them out as the mire of the streets.*
- Psalm 72:9: *They that dwell in the wilderness shall bow before him; And his enemies shall lick the dust.*
- Psalm 103:14: *For he knows our frame; He remembers that we are dust.*
- Psalm 119:25a: *My soul cleaves unto the dust.*

- Lamentations 3:29: *Let him put his mouth in the dust, if so be there may be hope.*
- Micah 1:10: *Tell it not in Gath, weep not at all: at Beth-le-aphrah have I rolled myself in the dust.*
- Revelation 18:19a: *And they cast dust on their heads, and cried.*

These verses show that dust is not considered to be anything valuable. Rather, it implies poverty or is used to show mourning and remorse.

Second, the fact that man was created from the ground is also a symbol of judgment, as the following verses indicate:
- Genesis 3:14: *And Jehovah God said unto the serpent, Because you have done this, cursed are you above all cattle, and above every beast of the field; upon your belly shall you go, and dust shall you eat all the days of your life.*
- Isaiah 65:25a: *The wolf and the lamb shall feed together, and the lion shall eat straw like the ox; and dust shall be the serpent's food.*

Third, the fact that man was formed from dust is also a symbol of death, as the following verses show:
- Genesis 3:19: *Dust you are, and unto dust shall you return.*
- Job 7:21b: *For now shall I lie down in the dust; And you will seek me diligently, but I shall not be.*
- Job 17:16: *It* [my hope] *shall go down to the bars of Sheol, When once there is rest in the dust.*
- Job 20:11: *His bones are full of his youth, But it shall lie down with him in the dust.*
- Job 21:26: *They lie down alike in the dust, And the worm covers them.*
- Psalm 22:15: *My strength is dried up like a potsherd; And my tongue cleaves to my jaws; And you have brought me into the dust of death.*
- Psalm 22:29: *All the fat ones of the earth shall eat and worship: All they that go down to the dust shall bow before him, Even he that cannot keep his soul alive.*

- Isaiah 26:19: *Your dead shall live; my dead bodies shall arise. Awake and sing, ye that dwell in the dust; for thy dew is as the dew of herbs, and the earth shall cast forth the dead.*
- Daniel 12:2: *And many of them that sleep in the dust of the earth shall awake, some to everlasting life, and some to shame and everlasting contempt.*

Genesis 2:7b deals with the creation of the immaterial part of man and more will be said about this in the next section.

In summary, Genesis 2:7a shows that while the material universe was created out of nothing (Gen. 2:4), the material part of man was created out of something, namely, *the dust of the ground*. Later in Genesis 3:19, God told Adam that as a result of the fall, he would return to dust upon death. This is the background of Paul's statement in I Corinthians 15:47-49 that the material part of man is *earthy* because it originated from the earth. While Adam was formed directly from the dust of the ground, Eve was made from his rib. Yet, ultimately, her origin is also dust because she was created out of Adam.

The origin of the material part of man also applies to the rest of humanity. Although all are born through the union of a man and a woman, they are descendants of the first couple and therefore also come from the dust of the ground. This truth shows the unity of the human race (Gen. 1:27-28; 2:7, 22; 3:20; 9:19 with 5:32; Acts 17:26-28; Rom. 5:12; I Cor. 15:21-22). The fact that the Bible emphasizes this unity militates against the theory of evolution, which requires several different strains of development.

## 1. The Transmission

The material part of man is transmitted from one generation to another through natural generation, meaning through the union of the female egg and the male sperm. Only Adam and Eve were divinely created from something. Only they had no ancestors. They were the only progenitors of the entire human race. From then on, all humankind has procreated through natural generation.

Sometimes people speak about God having created their baby, but in reality, He did not. The work of creation implies a work that only God can do, and yet scientists have succeeded in duplicating the fertilization of the female egg in a test tube. However, this is not an act of creation, but of natural generation. Again, only Adam and Eve were actually created by God. After that, the material part of man was passed on naturally from generation to generation through the union of the male sperm and the female egg.

## 2. The Designations

The material part of man is described in the Bible by seven designations. The first designation is the word "body." This term is used in four different ways in the Bible. The first is the word "body" itself (Mt. 6:22-23); most of the time, this term refers to the material part of man. A second use is "the body of sin" (Rom. 6:6), which emphasizes the power of the sin nature to express itself through the physical body. A third use is "the body of this death" (Rom. 7:24), which also emphasizes the sin nature's control over the body. The fourth use is "the body of our humiliation" (Phil. 3:21), which emphasizes the body in its unglorified state.

A second designation is the phrase "houses of clay" (Job 4:19). This expression emphasizes the origin of the body as having been created from the dust of the ground.

A third designation is the word "sheath" (Dan. 7:15). The point of this designation is that the immaterial part of man is the sword, and the material part of man is the sheath, which contains the sword.

A fourth designation for the material part of man is the word "flesh." In most cases, this term refers to the sin nature, but now and then, it is used of the physical part of man (I Cor. 15:39; Gal. 2:20; Col. 2:1, 5; I Tim. 3:16; I Pet. 3:18).

A fifth designation is the word "temple" (Jn. 2:21; I Cor. 6:19). This term only appears in the context of believers, whose bodies are temples in the sense that this is the place where God dwells.

A sixth designation is the expression "earthen vessels" (II Cor. 4:7), emphasizing the frailty of man.

A seventh designation is the word "tabernacle" (II Pet. 1:13-14), which emphasizes the temporary nature of the physical body.

## 3. The Future

Three things may be mentioned concerning the future of the material part of man. First, it is destined to be resurrected from the dead. There will be a resurrection of all believers and unbelievers alike (Jn. 5:28-29; Rom. 8:11; I Cor. 15:25-26).

Second, the body of the unbeliever will be cast alive into the lake of fire after this resurrection (Rev. 20:11-15).

Third, the body of the believer will have a better future. During their lifetime, believers undergo a process of sanctification that includes both their immaterial and material parts (I Thess. 5:23). Because they are undergoing this process of sanctification, believers are to glorify God in, by, and through their bodies (I Cor. 6:20). In the future, their bodies will be glorified (Rom. 8:18, 23; I Cor. 15:35-58; Phil. 3:20-21). The eternal abode of the believers' bodies will be the new Jerusalem (Rev. 21:1–22:5).

## 4. Summary

To summarize the material part of man: Adam was formed from the dust of the ground, and all humanity has its origin in Adam. After Adam, the material part of man was transmitted to each subsequent generation through natural procreation, that is, through the union of the female egg and the male sperm.

The Bible gives seven designations for the material part of man, calling it "body," "house of clay," "sheath," "flesh," "temple," "earthen vessel," and "tabernacle."

The future of the material part of man is threefold:
1. All people are destined to be resurrected.
2. The body of the unbeliever will be cast alive into the lake of fire.

3. The body of the believer will be sanctified and glorified and will dwell eternally in the new Jerusalem.

## B. The Immaterial Part of Man

### 1. The Origin

The origin of the immaterial part of man is God. The description of how man received his immaterial part is provided in Genesis 2:7: *And Jehovah God formed man of the dust of the ground, and breathed into his nostrils the breath of life; and man became a living soul.* The Hebrew term for "breath," *neshamah*, is used in the Scriptures twenty-five times for the breath of man (e.g., I Kgs. 17:17) and the breath of God (e.g., Job 4:9; 33:4; 34:14; Isa. 30:33). In Genesis 2:7, God's breath brings animation, causing man to become a living soul. It is this breath of God, the *neshamah,* that produced the life of man.

Job 34:14-15 notes that if God took back His Spirit and His breath, all flesh would perish together, and man would return to dust. Psalm 104:29 makes a similar point: *You hide your face, they are troubled; You take away their breath, they die, And return to their dust.* Isaiah 2:22 also mentions God's breath being in the nostrils of man: *Cease ye from man, whose breath is in his nostrils; for wherein is he to be accounted of?*

The *neshamah*, God's breath, involves both man and animal (Gen. 7:22). However, only to man is the breath of God given directly, making humanity distinct from the animal kingdom in that man is eternal, and animals are not eternal. The reason is that God's breath of life caused man to be *a living soul* (cf. I Cor. 15:45). This concept is also found in animals (Gen. 1:24, 30; 2:19). However, unlike animals, man is made in the image of God. Hence, his soul is far more complex than that of animals. Not only is man a physical being, but he is also spirit, and therefore eternal.

In summary, Genesis 2:7 teaches that the material part of man was divinely formed from the dust of the ground. The immaterial part of man originated with the breath of God. After God made the material part of man, He breathed His breath into the nostrils of this first human being. The result was that man became a living soul. The absence of the immaterial part means that the material part of man is dead (I Kgs. 17:21-22; Acts 2:27, 32).

## 2. The Transmission

The material part of man is transmitted from one generation to the next through natural generation by the union of the female egg and the male sperm. Three suggestions have been made as to how the immaterial part of man is transmitted.

### a. The Pre-existence of the Soul

The first suggestion is the pre-existence of the soul. It states that all the souls that have ever existed and will ever exist were created in the very beginning by God and enter the body either at conception or at birth. The doctrine further claims that the souls have a separate, conscious, personal existence in some previous state. Having sinned in that pervious state, they are condemned to be born into the world in a state of sin in connection with the material body.

This view was held by some of the church fathers, such as Origen. However, the Bible does not teach the pre-existence of the soul prior to the formation of the material part of man. Before we were conceived in the wombs of our mothers, neither our bodies nor our spirits existed. We simply did not exist at all. Of course, God knew that we would exist, but that is not the same as actually existing at some previous time.

### b. The Doctrine of Creationism

The second suggestion is known as the doctrine of creationism. It must be noted that in the context of the study of man's immaterial part, the term "creationism" does not refer to the theories regarding the origins of the world, the origins of man, or the age of the earth. Rather, the term deals with the origin and transmission of the soul.

As far as the immaterial part of man is concerned, creationism teaches that each soul is individually created *ex nihilo* ("out of nothing") and is placed into the body either at conception or at birth, or at some time in between.

Those who hold to this view believe it for three reasons. First, they point out that the body and soul are said to have different origins, with the soul coming from God. They cite any of the following verses to prove their point:

- Numbers 16:22, where God is called "the God of the spirits": *And they fell upon their faces, and said, O God, the God of the spirits of all flesh, shall one man sin, and will you be wroth with all the congregation?*
- Ecclesiastes 12:7, which states that the spirit returns to God who gave it: *and the dust returns to the earth as it was, and the spirit returns unto God who gave it.*
- Isaiah 42:5, which notes that God gives the spirit: *Thus says God Jehovah, he that created the heavens, and stretched them forth; he that spread abroad the earth and that which comes out of it; he that gives breath unto the people upon it, and spirit to them that walk therein.*
- Isaiah 57:16, which notes that God has made the souls: *For I will not contend for ever, neither will I be always wroth; for the spirit would faint before me, and the souls that I have made.*
- Zechariah 12:1b, which states that God forms the spirit of man within him: *Thus says Jehovah, who stretches forth the heavens, and lays the foundation of the earth, and forms the spirit of man within him.*
- Hebrews 12:9, which calls God "the Father of spirits": *Furthermore, we had the fathers of our flesh to chasten us, and we gave them reverence: shall we not much rather be in subjection unto the Father of spirits, and live?*

These verses are used in support of the argument that the body and the soul have different origins, with the soul coming from God.

In summary, the first reason to believe in the doctrine of creationism is that the soul is said to come from God. The second reason is that the nature of the soul is spiritual, and that which is spiritual must always come directly from God. The third reason is that this is the only way to explain why the Messiah did not have a sin nature.

In spite of these reasons for believing in the creationist's position on the origin of the immaterial part of man, this is not the best explanation of what the Bible really teaches. Five answers can be given to the creationist's claims. First, just like the soul, the body is also said to originate with God (Ps. 139:13-14; Jer. 1:5). When the Bible speaks of the body coming from God, it obviously points to its original source: God the Creator. However, God did not create the bodies after Adam and Eve. Rather, the material part of man is transmitted from generation to generation through natural procreation. When the Bible speaks of the soul coming from God, it could also refer to the ultimate origin of the soul, which is God's creation by the breath of His mouth. But this does not have to mean that every single soul is created by Him any more than every single body is formed by creation.

Second, the fact that the soul is spiritual does not exclude the possibility of its transmission through natural generation.

Third, the Messiah was not protected from the sin nature because God created a soul for Him, but because of the overshadowing of the Holy Spirit (Lk. 1:35).

Fourth, the creationist's view fails to explain why the soul tends to sin, unless God created the soul sinful. Those who hold this view do not teach that God created the soul sinful. But if God created the soul holy, why does it have a tendency to sin?

Fifth, according to this view, God creates the soul sinless, and then He puts the soul into a sinful body that, in turn, corrupts it. This concept causes a moral problem: How could God create a holy soul and then put it into a sinful body, knowing that upon contact, the body would corrupt the soul?

These five answers to the doctrine of creationism show that the Bible does not teach this view. God created Adam and Eve, and He created the first souls for Adam and Eve, but He does not create every individual soul any more than He creates every individual body.

## c. The Doctrine of Traducianism

The third suggestion for how the immaterial part of man is transmitted may be the best view. Theologically, it is called "traducianism," a term that comes from the Latin word *tradux*, meaning "vine branch." The derived meaning is "transmission" or "inheritance." According to traducianism, the immaterial part of man is transmitted through natural generation, just like the material part of man. At the point of conception, both parts are generated naturally.

Traducianism is the best view in light of Scripture for three reasons. First, Genesis 46:26 states that souls are already present in the loins: *All the souls that came with Jacob into Egypt, that came out of his loins, besides Jacob's sons' wives, all the souls were threescore and six.*

Second, according to Genesis 5:3, the begetting of a child includes the image and likeness of God: *And Adam lived a hundred and thirty years, and begat a son in his own likeness, after his image; and called his name Seth.* The image and likeness of God is not a component of the material part of man, but of the immaterial part of man. According to this verse, it is passed on to the next generation.

Third, the Bible teaches that the sin nature is already present at birth. Psalm 58:3, for example, states: *The wicked are estranged from the womb: They go astray as soon as they are born, speaking lies.* Other examples are Job 14:1-4; 15:14; and John 3:6. The sin nature that is already present at birth is a component of the immaterial part of man. Even more conclusive is the fact that, not only is the sin nature present at birth, but the sin nature is also present at conception, as David wrote in Psalm 51:5b: *in sin did my mother conceive me.* The sin nature, a facet of the immaterial part of man, is already present at conception.

The point is quite simple. Just as the material part of man is transmitted through natural generation, so too is the immaterial part of man transmitted through natural generation. At conception, both the material and immaterial parts of man are present. Therefore, biblically speaking, abortion is an act of murder, as it puts to death that which has been conceived, which includes both the material and immaterial parts of man.

## 3. The Trichotomy of Man

Trichotomy teaches a three-fold division of man: body, soul, and spirit. The body is the material part of man, and the soul and the spirit are thought to be two entirely separate entities of the immaterial part of man. While this has become a rather popular position, is this really what the Bible teaches?

Those who teach that man is trichotomous base their belief on three main passages. The first passage is I Thessalonians 5:23, which mentions the spirit, soul, and body: *And the God of peace himself sanctify you wholly; and may your spirit and soul and body be preserved entire, without blame at the coming of our Lord Yeshua Messiah.*

The second passage is I Corinthians 15:44, which seems to teach a sharp distinction between the soul and the spirit: *it is sown a natural body; it is raised a spiritual body. If there is a natural body, there is also a spiritual body.* The Greek term for "natural" is *psuchikos*, an adjective that is derived from the Greek noun *psuchei*, meaning "soul," "natural identity." So, *psuchikos* means "natural, of the soul or mind" and could be translated as "soulish." Hence, this verse seems to distinguish between the soulish body and the spiritual body.

The third passage is Hebrews 4:12: *For the word of God is living, and active, and sharper than any two-edged sword, and piercing even to the dividing of soul and spirit, of both joints and marrow, and quick to discern the thoughts and intents of the heart.* Here, the Word of God is said to divide the soul and the spirit of man.

However, when all that the Bible teaches concerning the composition of man is taken into account, it becomes clear that it does not support the view of a trichotomy in man. There are seven reasons why this is not the biblical view. First, while it is true that I Thessalonians 5:23 mentions spirit, soul, and body, there are other Scriptures that make different distinctions. For example, in Luke 10:27b, Messiah said: *You shall love the Lord your God with all your heart, and with all your soul, and with all your strength, and with all your mind; and your neighbor as yourself.* The verse mentions four elements: heart, soul, strength, and mind. In Mark 12:30, Yeshua also spoke of these four parts. If one applies the same principle of interpretation to Mark 12:30 and Luke 10:27 that is used in I Thessalonians 5:23, then man has four distinct parts, not three. However, what is really happening in Mark 12:30, Luke 10:27, and I Thessalonians 5:23 is that these verses paraphrase Deuteronomy 6:4-5, which teaches that one must love God with his entire being. Hence, the terms "heart," "soul," "strength," and "mind" stand for the whole man, including both his material and immaterial parts. In summary, while it is true that I Thessalonians 5:23 mentions three parts, other passages of Scripture make different divisions and mention other components as well. Therefore, the Thessalonian passage cannot be used to teach trichotomy.

Second, although I Corinthians 15:44 makes a distinction between the soulish body and the spiritual body, a careful contextual examination of the verse reveals that it is speaking about the physical body. The body is soulish; the same body is spiritual. Yet, no one thinks in terms of two bodies, only one. So, in answer to I Corinthians 15:44, the verse is not speaking of the immaterial part of man at all; it is speaking of the physical body.

Third, Hebrews 4:12 does indeed state that the Word of God can separate the soul and the spirit. However, this verse also states that the Word separates joints and marrow. Hence, if Hebrews 4:12 is used to teach a trichotomy in man composed of body, soul, and spirit, it should also be used to teach five parts: body, soul, spirit, and joints and marrow. However, what this verse really teaches is that there are only two parts to man. The joints and the marrow are simply facets of the material part of man, and the soul and the spirit are facets of the immaterial part of man. It is better to see man as having two parts, each part having many facets.

A fourth reason that a trichotomy in man is not the biblical view is that the terms "soul" and "spirit" are often used interchangeably, especially in the poetic portions of the Scriptures. For example, in Luke 1:46b-47, Miriam (Mary) said: *My soul does magnify the Lord, And my spirit has rejoiced in God my Saviour*. The principle of Hebrew poetry is not rhythm or rhyme but parallelism, in that the first line is followed by a second line that says the same thing using different words. Luke 1:46-47 is an example of a passage where "soul" and "spirit" are used interchangeably.

A fifth reason that a trichotomy in man is not a good position is that the terms "soul" and "spirit" are also used in reference to animals. For example, Ecclesiastes 3:21 states: *Who knows the spirit of man, whether it goes upward, and the spirit of the beast, whether it goes downward to the earth?* Here, the term "spirit" is used of animals. Revelation 16:3 uses the term "soul" of animals: *And the second poured out his bowl into the sea; and it became blood as of a dead man; and every living soul died, even the things that were in the sea*. Interestingly, those who believe in the trichotomy of man do not teach that animals are trichotomous. Consequently, the fact that the Scriptures use both "soul" and "spirit" of animals as well as of man proves that these two terms cannot be used to teach a trichotomy in man.

A sixth reason is derived from Genesis 2:7. The *nishemet hayim*, "the breath of life," mentioned in this verse as having been given to man is also seen in Genesis 6:17 and 7:21-22 in the context of animals. Furthermore, Genesis 2:7 describes man as *nephesh hayah*, "a living soul." The same Hebrew phrase is used in Genesis 1:21, 24, and 2:19 for animals. Hence, if Genesis 2:7 is used to teach a trichotomy in man, it must also teach a trichotomy in animals. But again, those who believe in a trichotomy in man do not believe in a trichotomy in animals. They are therefore inconsistent in their exegesis.

A seventh reason trichotomy cannot be the teaching of Scripture is that God is said to have a soul and a spirit. Regarding His soul, God said in Isaiah 42:1: *Behold, my servant, whom I uphold; my chosen, in whom my soul delights: I have put my Spirit upon him; he will bring forth justice to the Gentiles*. Other references that make the same point are Jeremiah 9:9; Amos 6:8; Matthew 12:18; and Hebrews 10:38. Regarding God's spirit, John 4:24 states: *God is a spirit: and they that worship him must worship in spirit and truth*. While everyone believes God is a trinity, no one believes that God is trichotomous. There are three different Persons in the Godhead, but God does not have three parts. Those who use the words "soul" and "spirit" to teach a trichotomy in man do not use them to teach a trichotomy in God. Yet, the Scriptures use these very terms to speak of God. Therefore, consistent exegesis contradicts the doctrine of a trichotomy in man. It is not correct to speak of man as being composed of three parts: body, soul, and spirit. Rather, man should be spoken of as being composed of two parts: material and immaterial, each part having various facets. This view is known as dichotomy.

## 4. The Dichotomy of Man

Dichotomy teaches a twofold division of man: material and immaterial, with each part having a number of facets. That this is the teaching of Scripture can be seen in four ways.

First, throughout the Scriptures, man is viewed as being composed of only two parts. The following verses are just a few examples of this teaching:
- Ecclesiastes 12:7: *and the dust returns to the earth as it was, and the spirit returns unto God who gave it*. In this verse, man is composed of dust, representing the body, and spirit.
- Isaiah 10:18: *And he will consume the glory of his forest, and of his fruitful field, both soul and body: and it shall be as when a*

*standard-bearer faints*. The two parts of man are the soul and the body.
- Daniel 7:15: *As for me, Daniel, my spirit was grieved in the midst of my body, and the visions of my head troubled me*. Again, spirit and body are listed as the parts of man.
- Matthew 10:28: *And be not afraid of them that kill the body, but are not able to kill the soul: but rather fear him who is able to destroy both soul and body in hell*. In this verse, Messiah mentioned the soul and the body of man.
- II Corinthians 4:16: *Wherefore we faint not; but though our outward man is decaying, yet our inward man is renewed day by day*. Paul distinguished between the outward man (the body) and the inward man (the soul).
- James 2:26: *For as the body apart from the spirit is dead, even so faith apart from works is dead*. James mentioned body and spirit as the two parts of man.

In these passages, man is consistently viewed as being composed of only two parts.

Second, that which God breathed into man was only one principle, and not two (Gen. 2:7; Job 27:3).

Third, the terms "soul" and "spirit" are not seen as distinct entities but are used interchangeably in Scripture. The same functions are ascribed to both the soul and the spirit. For example, they both get depressed (Gen. 41:8; Ps. 42:6) or troubled (Jn. 12:27; 13:21). Both are connected with the giving up of life (Mt. 20:28; 27:50). Both are seen as being in heaven (Heb. 12:23; Rev. 6:9). Both can glorify God (Lk. 1:46-47), and both were involved in the sacrifice of the Messiah (Jn. 10:15; 19:30). Another way of showing that the terms "soul" and "spirit" are used interchangeably in the Scriptures is that death is the giving up of either the soul or the spirit. Whether a person gives up his soul (Gen. 35:18; I Kg. 17:21; Acts 15:26) or his spirit (Ps. 31:5; Lk. 23:46; Acts 7:59), it is viewed as physical death. Finally, the interchangeability of these terms is seen in the fact that the dead are referred to by both names. Sometimes the dead are referred to as souls (Rev. 6:9; 20:4) and sometimes as spirits (Heb. 12:23; I Pet. 3:19).

Fourth, some passages proceed on the assumption that man consists of only two parts. In fact, these passages only make sense if they are understood as proceeding on this basis. Five passages may be listed as examples:

- Romans 8:10: *And if Messiah is in you, the body is dead because of sin; but the spirit is life because of righteousness*. This verse makes a clear distinction between the body and the spirit and proceeds to teach what it does on the assumption that man consists of only two parts.
- I Corinthians 5:5: *to deliver such a one unto Satan for the destruction of the flesh, that the spirit may be saved in the day of the Lord Yeshua*. This verse also proceeds to teach what it does on the assumption that man consists of only two parts: the body (referred to here as *the flesh*) and the spirit.
- I Corinthians 7:34b: *So also the woman that is unmarried and the virgin is careful for the things of the Lord, that she may be holy both in body and in spirit*. This verse is also based on the assumption that man has only two parts: the body and the spirit.
- II Corinthians 7:1: *Having therefore these promises, beloved, let us cleanse ourselves from all defilement of flesh and spirit, perfecting holiness in the fear of God*. Here again, there are only two parts to man: the flesh, which is used here of the physical part of man, and the spirit.
- Colossians 2:5a: *For though I am absent in the flesh, yet am I with you in the spirit*. Paul noted that he was absent in the flesh, that is, absent in the body. He was not with the believers physically, but he was with them in spirit. Only two parts of man are considered in this verse.

These five passages are examples of teachings that clearly proceed on the assumption that man consists of only two parts, not three.

To summarize the composition of man according to the doctrine of dichotomy, man is comprised of only two, not three parts. Man is comprised of a material and an immaterial part, and each part has a number of facets. Elements such as soul, spirit, heart, mind, bone, joints, and marrow are examples of facets of either the material part of man or the immaterial part of man. Of course, there are other facets to the material part of man, such as bone, blood, and skin. By the same token, the immaterial part of man has a number of facets as well. While the soul and spirit are not separate entities, they are two facets of the immaterial part of man.

## 5. The Seven Facets of the Immaterial Part of Man

### a. The Soul

The first facet of the immaterial part of man is the soul. The Hebrew word for soul is *nephesh*. It is used 754 times in the Scriptures, but it is not always translated as "soul." In fact, 45 different English words are used to translate this one Hebrew term, among which are "creature," "life," "self," "person," "mind," "heart," "will," "desire," "pleasure," "soul," and "life" (referring to both animal and human life).

The Greek word for soul is *psuchei*. It appears a total of 105 times in the Scriptures, and seven different English words are used to translate this one Greek term: 58 times as "soul," 40 times as "life," three times as "mind," once as "heart," once as "heartily," once as "us," and once as "you."

The Hebrew and Greek terms *nephesh* and *psuchei* are used in a number of different ways and translated into a number of different English words, showing that one cannot place a hard and fast meaning on the word "soul." The term emphasizes the non-material, personal being, and it is used in 16 different ways:

1. The term "soul" emphasizes man in his relationship to his body or earthly circumstances (Rev. 6:9; 20:4).
2. The term "soul" stands for the personal life of the individual (Jer. 31:25; I Pet. 2:11).

3. The term "soul" designates the breath of life that departs at death (Gen. 35:18; Job 33:18; Ps. 16:10; Is. 38:17).
4. The term "soul" designates the spirit of life that is embodied in the flesh (Ex. 21:23; Job 31:39).
5. The soul is the subject of all activities (Deut. 4:29; Ps. 42:2).
6. The individual who possesses life is viewed as a soul (Gen. 2:7; 14:21; 46:26-27; Num. 31:19; 35:15, 30; Deut. 27:25).
7. The soul is the center of one's mental activity (Lev. 26:11; Job 30:25; Ps. 42:2; Song 1:7).
8. The soul has the capacity to love God (Mt. 22:37).
9. The soul needs watching (Heb. 13:17).
10. The soul can stand against the works of the flesh (I Pet. 2:11).
11. The natural or soulish man is viewed as the unsaved man (I Cor. 2:14; Jude 19).
12. The natural or soulish body is the un-resurrected body (I Cor. 15:44).
13. The soul is included in the process of sanctification (I Thess. 5:23).
14. The soul has the capacity to glorify God (Lk. 1:46).
15. The soul needs to be laid bare by the Word of God (Heb. 4:12).
16. The soul was involved in the sacrifice of the Messiah (Jn. 10:15).

To summarize this facet of the immaterial part of man, one cannot place a hard and fast meaning on the word "soul" other than to say that the term emphasizes the non-material, personal being.

## b. The Spirit

The second facet of the immaterial part of man is the spirit. The Hebrew word for "spirit" is *ruach*, and the Greek term is *pneuma*. The term "spirit" emphasizes the non-material, personal being in relationship to God (Jn. 4:24; Heb. 12:23; I Pet. 3:18-20).

Like the term "soul," the word "spirit" is used in a number of different ways:

1. The term "spirit" is related to the higher aspects of man, such as witnessing and giving assurance (Rom. 8:16).

2. The spirit is the principle of life (Lk. 23:46; Acts 7:59; I Cor. 5:5).
3. All men have a spirit, because the absence of the spirit means physical death (I Cor. 2:11; Jas. 2:26).
4. The spirit can be corrupted (II Cor. 7:1).
5. The spirit is the seat of the emotions (Gen. 45:27; Num. 5:14; Ps. 51:17; 143:4; Prov. 15:13; Eccl. 7:8; Mt. 5:3; Rom. 8:15; 11:8; Gal. 6:1; II Tim. 1:7).
6. The spirit is the source of both life and death (Job 27:3; 33:4; 34:14).
7. The spirit is the inner life of man (Mt. 5:3; I Cor. 2:11).
8. The spirit is God-derived life (Ps. 51:10; Is. 26:9).
9. The term "spirit" is synonymous with "the new nature" (Rom. 8:6, 10).
10. Spiritual sacrifices and singing are related to the spirit (Col. 3:16; I Pet. 2:5).
11. The spiritual man is the one who is rightly related to God (I Cor. 2:15).
12. The spiritual body is the resurrected body (I Cor. 15:44).
13. The spirit is included in the process of sanctification (I Thess. 5:23).
14. The spirit has the capacity to glorify God (Lk. 1:47).
15. The spirit can partake of corruption (II Cor. 7:1).
16. The spirit needs to be laid bare by the Word of God (Heb. 4:12).
17. The spirit was also involved in the sacrifice of the Messiah (Jn. 19:30).

Many of the things that are true of the spirit of man are also true of the soul of man. Therefore, one cannot make a sharp distinction between the two terms. Rather, because the soul and the spirit are not separate and distinct entities, the terms are used interchangeably, and there is an overlap. Both the spirit and the soul are facets of the immaterial part of man.

## c. The Heart

The third facet of the immaterial part of man is the heart. The Hebrew word used in the Scriptures is *lev*, and the Greek word is *kardia*.

The term "heart" is used in three different senses in the Scriptures. First, it is used twice of the physical heart as the seat of physical life (II Sam. 18:14; II Kg. 9:24).

Second, it is used metaphorically as the middle or the inner part of something. An example of this usage is found in Exodus 15:8b, which speaks of the heart of the sea: *The deeps were congealed in the heart of the sea*. Here, the phrase "heart of the sea" refers to the middle or inner part of the sea. Another example is Deuteronomy 4:11, which speaks of the heart of heaven: *And ye came near and stood under the mountain; and the mountain burned with fire unto the heart of heaven, with darkness, cloud, and thick darkness*. The phrase "heart of heaven" refers to the middle or inner part of heaven. A third example is Matthew 12:40, which mentions the heart of the earth: *for as Jonah was three days and three nights in the belly of the whale; so shall the Son of man be three days and three nights in the heart of the earth*. The phrase "heart of the earth" refers to the middle or inner part of the earth.

Third, the term "heart" is used as a facet of the immaterial part of man. With over 700 examples, this is the most common usage of the term in the Scriptures. It contains the broadest concepts of all the facets of man's immaterial nature.

The usage of the term "heart" can be divided into five categories:
1. The term "heart" is used as the seat of the intellectual life. In this sense, it is often a synonym for the word "mind." For example, the Bible speaks about the imagination of the thoughts of the heart (Gen. 6:5); the thoughts and intents of the heart (Heb. 4:12); evil thoughts of the heart (Mt. 15:19); and the heart as the place, where the believer hides his knowledge of the Word of God (Ps. 119:11).
2. The term "heart" is used as the seat of the emotional life. The heart has the capacity to love (Deut. 6:5), to desire (Ps. 37:4),

to rejoice (Ps. 104:15), to be bitter (Prov. 14:10), and to be filled with sorrow (Rom. 9:2).
3. It is used as the seat of the volitional life. In this sense, it is often a synonym for the word "will." The heart is able to choose (Ex. 7:23), to turn aside (Ex. 14:5), to seek (Deut. 4:29), and to purpose (II Cor. 9:7). One can harden his heart (Ex. 8:15).
4. The term "heart" is used as the seat of the spiritual life. Isaiah 6:10 and Hebrews 4:7 speak of a heart hardened to spiritual truth. On the other hand, Ezekiel 36:26 speaks of a new heart, one that is open to God's input.
5. The term "heart" is used as the seat of sin, meaning the place where sin resides (Gen. 8:21).

The Bible clearly distinguishes the heart of the unbeliever from the heart of the believer. Among the things the Bible teaches concerning the heart of the unbeliever is that his heart is evil (Jer. 3:17), desperately wicked and deceptive (Jer. 17:9), uncircumcised (Acts 7:51), hard and unrepentant (Rom. 2:5), hardened so that it cannot receive spiritual truth (Eph. 4:18), and deceived (Jas. 1:26).

On the other hand, when a person becomes a believer, he gains a new nature that has a new heart. The new heart can do all those things that the unbelieving heart is incapable of doing. The heart of the believer has the capacity to love God (Mt. 22:37). It is circumcised (Rom. 2:29). It has the love of God spread abroad (Rom. 5:5). It is obedient (Rom. 6:17). It believes unto righteousness (Rom. 10:10). It is the place where the Holy Spirit resides (II Cor. 1:22), and it is the place where the Messiah resides (Eph. 3:17). Nevertheless, even the heart of the believer could become hardened (Heb. 3:8, 12-13). The writer of the book of Hebrews is clearly speaking to believers when he warns them against hardening their hearts, but he encourages them to make sure their hearts are both true and pure (Heb. 10:22).

Because of the broad usage of the term "heart," this facet of man's immaterial part covers some of the aspects of the soul and the spirit, as well as aspects of conscience and will, to be discussed later. This shows that one must not divide these facets into separate and distinct categories, for all of the facets that comprise the immaterial part of man overlap with each other.

To summarize the facet of the heart, its usage is divided into five categories: The heart is the seat of the intellectual life, the emotional life, the volitional life, the spiritual life, and sin. Furthermore, the Bible describes the heart of the unbeliever as being evil, desperately wicked, deceptive, uncircumcised, hard, unrepentant, unable to receive spiritual truth, and deceived. The heart of the believer is characterized as being a new heart that has the capacity to love God, is circumcised, is obedient, believes unto righteousness, and is the place where the Messiah resides. Nevertheless, the heart of the believer can become hardened.

### d. The Flesh

The fourth facet of the immaterial part of man is the flesh. The Hebrew word for this facet is *basar*, and the Greek word is *sarx*.

In both Hebrew and Greek, there are two main categories in which the term "flesh" is used. First, it is used of the material part of man as a reference to the skin or the physical body as a whole (Gen. 2:24; 6:3; 7:21; 29:14; Job 19:26; Ps. 56:4; 63:1; Mt. 16:17; 26:41; Jn. 1:14; Acts 2:31; I Cor. 15:39, 50; I Tim. 3:16; Heb. 5:7).

Second, the term "flesh" is used to describe the immaterial part of man. In this category, the term is used in four ways. First, it is sometimes used in reference to the sin nature (Rom. 7:18).

Second, the flesh dwells within the immaterial part of man as a result of the fall and will affect all other facets (Rom. 8:1-11; Gal. 5:16-21).

Third, when God created Adam and Eve, they had a soul, spirit, heart, mind, conscience, and will. However, they did not have the flesh. Only as a result of their fall did this facet become an integral component of the immaterial part of man. Consequently, the flesh is viewed as being completely corrupt and something that cannot be renewed. All the other facets of man's immaterial nature are renewed in the believer, except this one. For that reason, the flesh will be eradicated upon death or at the rapture, while the other six facets will be there for all eternity.

Fourth, the word "flesh" is used as a reference to the immaterial part of man in that it can be defined as the capacity to serve self. The flesh is the ability to do all those things, good or bad, that can in no way commend one to God.

As mentioned, the term "flesh" is sometimes used in reference to the sin nature. The expression "sin nature" is not found in the Bible. It is a theological term that is meant to describe a concept found in the Scriptures. The Bible gives the term "flesh" another name: "the old man" (Rom. 6:6; Eph. 4:22; Col. 3:9). This name points to the origin of the flesh, which is Adam and his fall into sin. The word "flesh" emphasizes the sin nature itself, while the expression "old man" emphasizes its origin: Adam's original sin.

In relation to this particular facet, the Bible distinguishes the unbeliever from the believer. Concerning the unbeliever, the flesh is the only nature he has. Everything he does in life is based on the flesh, on the sin nature. He is always in opposition to God and His holiness. He has no other option, for everything he does or does not do, either good or bad, is done on the basis of the sin nature alone (Rom. 8:5-13; Gal. 5:16-17; Col. 2:11; I Pet. 2:11; Jude 23).

The believer has a different status. When a person becomes a believer, he still retains his sin nature. The sin nature is not eradicated upon salvation, but will only be eradicated at death or at the rapture. However, in addition to his old nature, the believer has a new nature dwelling inside the immaterial part of him. Just as the old nature impacts the other facets, this new nature also affects all the other facets. Hence, the believer has a choice. He can either do things or not do things on the basis of the old nature or the new nature. The new nature is the capacity to serve God with righteousness (Rom. 6:18-20). The source of the new nature is God (Col. 3:10; II Pet. 1:4). Therefore, the new nature is given another designation: "the new man" (Eph. 4:22-24; Col. 3:9-10). The old nature is the old man; the new nature is the new man. Because the old nature cannot be renewed, it is necessary to create a new nature in the believer, and that is why this new nature is called "the new man." Because the believer has both natures, there is a conflict within him. This conflict is described in Romans 7:15-25 and Galatians 5:16-17. The picture is that these two natures are in a continuous struggle for the acts of the believer. The believer is encouraged to walk on the basis of his new nature and is discouraged from walking on the basis of the old nature or the flesh.

To summarize the flesh as a facet of the immaterial part of man, the term "flesh" is used either in reference to the physical body or in reference to the immaterial part of man. If used in reference to the immaterial part of man, the term is a synonym for the sin nature. The flesh dwells within the immaterial part of man. It is completely corrupt and cannot be renewed. It has the capacity to serve self. The biblical term for the concept of the sin nature is "the old man." This is the only nature unbelievers possess, and everything they do is done on the basis of the sin nature. In contrast to the unbeliever, the believer is given a new nature called "the new man," which has the capacity to serve God with righteousness. The believer has the option to walk on the basis of the new man.

### e. The Mind

The fifth facet of the immaterial part of man is the mind. The Scriptures use two basic Greek terms, both of which are translated by the English word "mind." The first term is *nous*, meaning "mind," "understanding," and "reason." It refers to the God-given capacity of man to think and describes man as a cognitive thinker. It emphasizes the inwardness of one's mental aptitude. *Nous* is found in passages such as Luke 24:45, Romans 7:25, and I Corinthians 14:15. Related to this Greek term is *dianoia* (Lk. 10:27), meaning "the mind." Another related term is *ennoia* (I Pet. 4:1), meaning "thinking," "thoughtfulness, i.e. moral understanding." The second basic Greek term is *phren* (I Cor. 14:20), meaning "midriff," "heart," "mind," and "thought." The term refers to deep reflection and emphasizes man as a deep, reflective, and meditative thinker. Related to this term is *phronéma* (Rom. 8:6-7, 27), which means "the thought (that which is in the mind)."

The mind is the facet of the immaterial part of man in which the understanding is centered. It is the seat of the intellectual life. This facet has been affected and marred by the fall, but the mind of the believer can be renewed in the Messiah (Rom. 12:2; Eph. 4:22-24).

As with some of the other facets, the Bible distinguishes between the mind of the unbeliever and the mind of the believer. The mind of the unbeliever is described as being evil (Gen. 6:5), reprobate (Rom. 1:26), unable to understand the things of God (Rom. 3:11), at war with God (Rom. 8:6-7), blinded by Satan (II Cor. 4:4), darkened and vain or empty (Eph. 4:17-18), corrupt (I Tim. 6:5), and defiled (Tit. 1:15). Because the unbeliever's mind is at war with God, it must develop intellectual arguments against the truth of God. It is the unregenerate mind that produced theories about the origin of man that exclude God. It was the mind of the unbeliever that invented explanations concerning the origin of the universe in order to circumvent the biblical creation account. In fact, the unbeliever experiences intellectual conflict in every area. In philosophy, the unbeliever thinks of philosophical arguments against Scripture; in sociology, there are sociological arguments that contradict the biblical message; in science, there are scientific arguments. The mind of the unbeliever must devise alternatives to biblical teaching because, if the Bible is true and if there really is a God, then man is responsible to that God. The mind of the unbeliever does not wish to submit itself to the authority of the Creator, so the unbeliever must invent different forms of argumentation. He must think up different theories to explain the origin of man and the purpose of life so that he can do away with God intellectually. Then he will have no sense of responsibility to this Creator.

Man has become vain in his understanding. His mind has become corrupt and reprobate, which, in turn, has led to immorality (Rom. 1:22-32). When man found ways to do away with God by offering alternative explanations for the origin of the universe, the next step was indeed immorality. For that reason, believers must bring down strongholds against the truth of God. They are encouraged to use their minds to counter the arguments that unbelievers raise against the biblical account of the Creator and the creature.

The mind of the believer is to be different than the mind of the unbeliever. It is not to think too highly of itself because that could lead to pride (Rom. 12:3; Phil. 2:5). It has the capacity to love God (Mt. 22:37). It is enlightened so that it can understand spiritual truth (Lk. 24:45). It can serve the law of God (Rom. 7:25). It can arrive at proper conclusions in the area of amoral (meaning non-moral) issues (Rom. 14:5). It is to reflect the mind of the Messiah (I Cor. 2:16). Lastly, it is by means of the mind that the believer can understand the will of God (Eph. 5:17).

In I Peter 1:13, the believer is encouraged to capture the mind so that it does not have any undisciplined thoughts. This concept is also taught by II Corinthians 10:5, which states that the believer must bring every thought into captivity to the obedience of the Messiah. The thought life, which is a product of the mind, must be put into total subjection to God.

The formula for capturing every thought is twofold. First is the renewing of the mind, which entails memorizing Scripture (Rom. 12:2; Eph. 4:23; Col. 3:10). The minds of unbelievers are being programmed by the world. Hence, when a person comes to faith, he is to stop the process and needs to allow God's Word to renew or reprogram his mind by means of memorizing Scripture and meditating upon Scripture. The renewed mind will think the way God is thinking, and the biblical principles one has memorized will transition from the mind to the heart. The believer's lifestyle will conform accordingly.

Second, there are certain things believers should be focusing on. These are listed in Philippians 4:8: *Finally, brethren, whatsoever things are true, whatsoever things are honorable, whatsoever things are just, whatsoever things are pure, whatsoever things are lovely, whatsoever things are of good report; if there be any virtue, and if there be any praise, think on these things.* While much of what passes for "positive thinking" today is not biblical, this verse presents a form of biblical positive thinking. Paul mentioned several positive things that the believer should concentrate on. By doing so, it will be possible for the believer to bring every thought into captive obedience to the Messiah.

To summarize, the mind, being a facet of the immaterial part of man, is the seat of the intellectual life that has been marred by the fall. The mind of the unbeliever is described as being evil, reprobate, unable to understand the things of God, at war with God, blinded by Satan, darkened, vain, corrupt, and defiled. It cannot be renewed. The mind of the believer is different. It does not think too highly of itself, has the capacity to love God, is enlightened, is able to serve the law of God, is able to arrive at proper conclusions, reflects the mind of the Messiah, is able to understand the will of God, and can be renewed by means of memorizing and mediating on the Word of God.

### f. The Will

The sixth facet of the immaterial part of man is the will. The Hebrew word for "will" is *ratzon* (e.g., Gen. 49:6; Ex. 28:38), and the Greek word is *theléma* (e.g., Mt. 6:10; 18:14; Acts 13:22). Both of these terms emphasize the non-material being in its cognitive aspect and activity. The term "will" involves the aspect of putting forth effort and making choices. The will is the power of man's immaterial part to choose between motives and to direct its subsequent activities according to the motives it has chosen. The will is man's power to choose between ends and the means of obtaining these ends. He could choose legitimate means to attain legitimate ends, or he could use illegitimate means to attain either legitimate or illegitimate ends.

The Bible distinguishes the will of the unbeliever from the will of the believer. The will of an unbeliever can do good things (Acts 27:43). However, it willfully forgets what God has done (II Pet. 3:5).

The will of the believer is radically different. Romans 7:15-25 speaks of the believer's will in action in the area of contrary choice. This passage describes the two natures, or the two capacities, struggling within the believer for control. Regardless of how the believer chooses to act, whether on the basis of the old or the new nature, he is acting on the basis of his will.

According to I Corinthians 7:36-39, the will of the believer can make a choice from several possibilities, all of which would be right. It is wrong to teach that there is only one perfect will of God in every area for the believer. In fact, in order to determine what is God's will, one must first investigate all possibilities and then exclude those options that are clearly contrary to Scripture. Suppose that the believer has five options, but two of them would require him to act contrary to Scripture. These two options would automatically be eliminated, but the other three would still be valid choices. Any one of those three remaining choices will be fine with God. In this case, the believer should use his renewed will to make the choice that he needs to make, based on the wisdom available to his renewed mind.

Philippians 2:13 teaches that God's will is worked out through the believer's will: *for it is God who works in you both to will and to work, for his good pleasure*. By means of His Word, God guides the believer in making proper choices. Titus 3:8b teaches that the will of the believer allows him to do what is right: *they who have believed God may be careful to maintain good works. These things are good and profitable unto men*. On the other hand, the believer's will may lead him to choose that which is wrong. Hence, in the area of the will, the believer can choose to do either right or wrong (I Tim. 6:9; Jas. 4:4).

The basic thrust of what the Bible teaches concerning the believer's will is this: What I do, I have willed to do. Therefore, I am responsible. One cannot simply say, "The devil made me do it." While the enemy may put a temptation in front of a believer, submission to that temptation is a matter of the will. The believer who sins has chosen to fall to that temptation, for he could have resisted Satan to the point that he would flee (Jas. 4:7).

To summarize, the will, being a facet of the immaterial part of man, has the power to choose between motives and to direct the mind's subsequent activity to attain either legitimate or illegitimate ends. The will of the unbeliever can do good things, but it forgets what God has done. The will of the believer can act on the basis of his old nature or his new nature, and it can determine the will of God by means of His Word.

### g. The Conscience

The seventh and final facet of the immaterial part of man is the conscience. The Hebrew Bible does not have a special word that means "conscience." It only covers the concept of man's conscience by the facet of the heart. Two passages where the term "heart" is used in the sense of conscience are II Samuel 24:10 and Job 27:6. In the Greek New Testament, the term for "conscience" is *suneidésis*. The word combines the Greek terms *sýn* ("together with") and *eídō* ("to know, see"). Hence, a literal translation of *suneidésis* would be "joint-knowing." Conscience joins moral and spiritual knowledge. It is the God-given capacity to know right from wrong. It is an innate discernment, a self-judging knowledge. Most people possess a conscience because they are free moral agents.[55]

This definition of the Greek term *suneidésis* allows one to make four general statements regarding conscience. First, knowledge and conscience go together. The knowledge a person possesses enables his conscience to guide him in one direction or another. Hence, conscience is the application of knowledge to a special act.

Second, conscience is knowledge about oneself (including one's actions and states) in the context of a moral norm or law. A person has knowledge of what the law says. He is aware of a certain moral standard. When he fails to obey this law or when he fails to conform to this moral standard, his conscience begins to act.

Third, the conscience reveals whether or not acts conform to a given standard.

Fourth, the conscience judges according to the standard given to it. If the standard itself is wrong, then the conscience will be wrong; if

---

[55] More will be said about free agency in Chapter VIII.

the standard is right, the conscience will be right. The only true standard of judgment is the Word of God.

Like the mind, the conscience of man has been affected by the fall. It is a marred conscience, but it can still be a safe witness (Heb. 10:22; I Pet. 2:19).

The Bible speaks about nine different types of conscience:
1. There is an evil conscience (Heb. 10:22).
2. There is a good conscience (Acts 23:1; I Tim. 1:5,19; Heb. 13:18; I Pet. 3:16-21).
3. There is a weak conscience (I Cor. 8:7-12).
4. There is a strong conscience (I Cor. 8:7-12; I Cor. 10:25-29).
5. There is a defiled conscience (I Cor. 8:7; Tit. 1:15).
6. There is a wounded conscience (I Cor. 8:12).
7. There is a seared conscience, one that is no longer able to guide at all (I Tim. 4:2).
8. There is a pure conscience, one that can do what a seared conscience cannot do (II Tim. 1:3).
9. There is a conscience void of offense (Acts 24:16).

Because the conscience of man has been marred by the fall, it is not an absolute guide. If the standard on which it operates is faulty, the conscience will also be faulty. For example, suppose someone has been taught that drinking Coca Cola or coffee is a sin, and that is the standard under which he has been raised, his conscience will bother him whenever he drinks a glass of Coke or a cup of coffee. His conscience is wrong. It is a weak conscience, because it is based on a wrong standard, for the Bible does not teach that drinking coffee or Coca Cola is a sin. Therefore, only if one operates on the basis of the correct standard, i.e., the Word of God, is the conscience a proper guide.

Another thing regarding the biblical teaching on conscience is that it has certain dispensational aspects. Under the dispensation of law, the believer had his sins forgiven and covered, but his conscience was not cleansed (Heb. 9:9; 10:2). Under the dispensation of grace, the believer not only has his sins forgiven, but his conscience is also cleansed (Heb. 9:14; 10:22).

The main work of the conscience is to bear witness to the true standard (Rom. 2:15; 9:1). The Bible mentions seven things that the conscience can or should do:
1. Being obedient to the government is a matter of conscience (Rom. 13:5).
2. Doing a good job for an unworthy employer is a matter of conscience (I Pet. 2:19).
3. The conscience should test the quality of the believer's testimony for the Lord (II Cor. 1:12).
4. The consciences of others should agree that it is a proper testimony (II Cor. 4:2).
5. The conscience should attest to the truth of one's claims (Rom. 9:1).
6. The conscience is a guide to social activities in relationship to other believers (I Cor. 8:7-12).
7. The conscience is the basis on which believers are to endure trials (I Pet. 2:19).

Believers who abide by the above standards will enjoy a good conscience.

To summarize conscience as a facet of the immaterial part of man, conscience and knowledge go together. Conscience is the understanding of self and one's actions in relation to a moral standard. It was marred by the fall. Therefore, conscience can be a reliable guide only if it acts on the right standard, the Word of God.

## C. The Relationship Between the Material and the Immaterial

The relationship between the material and the immaterial part of man is a vital union. The immaterial part of man is the source of life for the material part.

Certain states of man's material part produce corresponding states in the immaterial part. For example, the immaterial part of man often operates on the basis of the five senses of man's material part.

Furthermore, some actions of the material part of man are dependent on the immaterial part. For example, physical activities are dependent on man's will to engage in these activities. The will is a facet of the immaterial part of man, while physical actions are a facet of the material part of man. Other actions of the material part are not dependent upon the immaterial. For example, the liver, heart, and lung operate independently of the immaterial parts of man.

There is a realistic dualism in that the material and the immaterial are distinct parts that do interact, though their mode of interaction is not clearly known at this time. The union between the two may be called "a union of life," with both acting on the other.

## D. Questions and Study Suggestions

*Question 1:* Read Genesis 1:27-28; 2:7, 22; 3:20; 9:19; Acts 17:26-28; Romans 5:12; and I Corinthians 15:21-22. What do these Scriptures teach us about the unity of the human race?

*Question 2:* According to John 5:28-29, what is the future of every human body?

*Question 3:* What is the origin of man's immaterial part?

*Question 4:* Do human beings have two or three parts?

*Question 5:* Does the unbeliever have the capacity to serve God? If your answer is no, why not?

*Question 6:* According to the Bible, what is the mind of man?

*Question 7:* What is the will of man?

*Question 8:* Read Hebrews 9:9, 14; 10:2, 22. What do these verses teach us about man's conscience in the different dispensations?

*Study Suggestion 1:* Read I Corinthians 15:47-49 and explain the material part of man.

*Study Suggestion 2:* According to the Scriptures, the heart is the seat of the _____ life, the _____ life, the _____ life, the _____ life, and of _____.

*Study Suggestion 3:* Explain the relationship between the material and the immaterial parts of man.

## Chapter VI:
# The Fall of Man

The fall of man will be dealt with in four categories: the state of innocence, the temptation, the fall, and the results.

## A. The State of Innocence

Man's original state before the fall is called "the state of innocence." There are four aspects to this state: man's unconfirmed holiness, his power of contrary choice, his dominion over creation, and his fellowship with God.

### 1. Man's Unconfirmed Holiness

Man was created in a state of maturity and perfection. He possessed original righteousness and the image of God. His original righteousness involved three things: First, there was perfect harmony and subordination of all that constituted man; second, this righteousness included knowledge and holiness (Eph. 4:24; Col. 3:10); and third, it included passive moral qualities, meaning that in his original state, man was innocent of any wrongdoing. Theologically, this condition is called "unconfirmed, creaturely holiness," an expression that was mentioned in previous chapters. Man was created holy, but that holiness had not yet been tested. It was unconfirmed. Furthermore, it was not the holiness of the Creator, who does not have the capacity to sin, but creaturely holiness, meaning a holiness that included the capacity to disobey and sin. In summary, Adam was created in a state of unconfirmed, creaturely holiness. He had an innocent moral character that had not yet been tested.

As to the image of God in man, this concept includes certain facets of the outward image of God as well as the inward image. The outward image of God includes that man has the capacity for facial expressions, that he has speech, and that he can exercise dominion. The inward image of God in man includes aspects such as immortality, intellect, self-consciousness, the ability to reason, emotions, will, morality, and spirituality.

Four additional things should be noted regarding the image of God in man. First, the expression refers to those features of God that are also true of man. Second, there is one feature that no longer exists, and that is unconfirmed creaturely holiness, which was lost in the fall. Third, even after the fall, God and man continue to share other features. The content of the image of God in man is not a physical likeness, but a personal likeness, a spiritual likeness, a moral likeness, a social likeness, and an authoritative likeness. Man still has the image of God in him, but it is marred. Fourth, although the image of God is marred, there is still enough of it left in man that every person is commanded to respect his or her neighbor accordingly.

## 2. Man's Power of Contrary Choice

When Adam was created in a state of innocence, he had the ability to sin or not to sin. Theologically, this is called "the power of contrary choice," the ability to choose contrary to one's nature. Adam was holy and perfect, but he had the capacity to make an unholy and imperfect choice. God does not have this ability.

The Bible clearly teaches that the nature of God is such that He is incapable of sinning. Habakkuk 1:13 shows that God is holy, absolute pure, and separated from evil: *You that are of purer eyes than to behold evil, and that cannot look on perverseness, wherefore look you upon them that deal treacherously, and hold your peace when the wicked swallows up the man that is more righteous than he.* Psalm

11:7 speaks of God's righteousness, or justice: *For Jehovah is righteous; he loves righteousness: The upright shall behold his face.* Titus 1:2 notes God's truthfulness: *in hope of eternal life, which God, who cannot lie, promised before times eternal.* This is only a very brief description of some of God's attributes. God is holy, just, and true, and He is incapable of doing anything inconsistent with Himself. Because God is "holy, holy, holy" (Isa. 6:3), He is incapable of doing anything unholy. Therefore, if He were to sin, He would cease to be God. But Adam, in his original state, had the ability to sin or not to sin.

### 3. Man's Dominion over Creation

When man was created in the state of innocence, he was given dominion over creation as a consequence of having been formed in the image of God. Originally, it was Satan who had this authority over the earth (Ezek. 28:11-19), but he lost it when he fell.[56] As a result, God created a new race of beings, man, to whom He gave this dominion. The specific areas of man's dominion include the animal kingdom (Gen. 1:26b, 28) and the material earth (Gen. 1:26c).

Passages that speak of man's dominion include Genesis 1:26, Psalm 8:5-8, and Hebrews 2:5-8:

- Genesis 1:26: *And God said, Let us make man in our image, after our likeness: and let them have dominion over the fish of the sea, and over the birds of the heavens, and over the cattle, and over all the earth, and over every creeping thing that creeps upon the earth.*
- Psalm 8:5-8: *[5]For you have made him but little lower than God, And crown him with glory and honor. [6]You make him to have dominion over the works of your hands; You have put all things under his feet: [7]All sheep and oxen, Yea, and the beasts of the*

---

[56] For details regarding Satan's fall, see: Arnold G. Fruchtenbaum, *A Study of the Angelic Realm: Angelology, Satanology, and Demonology* (San Antonio, TX: Ariel Ministries, 2020).

*field, ⁸The birds of the heavens, and the fish of the sea, Whatsoever passes through the paths of the seas.*
- Hebrews 2:5-8: *⁵For not unto angels did he subject the world to come, whereof we speak. ⁶But one has somewhere testified, saying, What is man, that you are mindful of him? Or the son of man, that you visit him? ⁷You made him a little lower than the angels; You crowned him with glory and honor, And did set him over the works of your hands: ⁸You did put all things in subjection under his feet. For in that he subjected all things unto him, he left nothing that is not subject to him. But now we see not yet all things subjected to him.*

Adam was given authority over the earth. He had dominion over creation. The naming of the animals, described in Genesis 2:20a, was the first exercise of this dominion: *And the man gave names to all cattle, and to the birds of the heavens, and to every beast of the field.*

### 4. Man's Fellowship with God

When man was created in the state of innocence, he was in fellowship with God. This point is brought out in Genesis 3:8a: *And they heard the voice of Jehovah God walking in the garden in the cool of the day.* Every day when the sun was setting, God would appear in some visible way to Adam and Eve and fellowship with them. Hence, in his original state of innocence, man had unbroken fellowship with God, which was exercised in a meeting face to face, regularly, on a day-by-day basis.

## B. Man's Original Environment and Responsibilities

Man's original environment during the state of innocence is described in Genesis 2:8-15:

*⁸And Jehovah God planted a garden eastward, in Eden; and there he put the man whom he had formed. ⁹And out of the ground made Jehovah God to grow every tree that is pleasant to the*

## The Fall of Man

> *sight, and good for food; the tree of life also in the midst of the garden, and the tree of the knowledge of good and evil. ¹⁰And a river went out of Eden to water the garden; and from thence it was parted, and became four heads. 11The name of the first is Pishon: that is it which compasses the whole land of Havilah, where there is gold; ¹²and the gold of that land is good: there is bdellium and the onyx stone. ¹³And the name of the second river is Gihon: the same is it that compasses the whole land of Cush. ¹⁴And the name of the third river is Hiddekel: that is it which goes in front of Assyria. And the fourth river is the Euphrates. ¹⁵And Jehovah God took the man, and put him into the garden of Eden to dress it and to keep it.*

When man was created, he was put in the Garden of Eden. In this environment, there were plenty of provisions that sustained Adam and Eve. There were various fruit trees, and there was also the tree of life to sustain life itself.

Labor was part of the original environment. In his state of innocence, man had a responsibility that can be summarized in two points: First, he was obligated to *dress* and *keep* the Garden of Eden; and second, he was to obey God. The Hebrew term for "dress," *avad*, means "to work" or "to serve." It emphasizes physical activity. The term is also used for work in the service of God. Hence, man's first physical activity was a spiritual service to God. Man was in the garden not to be served but to be a servant. The Hebrew term for "keep," *shamar*, means "to watch" and "preserve." The same word is used in Genesis 3:24, where the Cherubim were given to guard the entryway to the Garden of Eden. Keeping the garden in the sense of guarding it would be an act of obedience. The emphasis here is that Adam was to guard the Garden of Eden, not to protect it from external attacks but to guard it in the sense of obeying the commandment of God. In summary, labor was part of the perfect state of man. However, it was not toilsome. It was necessary, but light and enjoyable work.

As to man's obedience, Genesis 2:16-17 adds the following directions:

> ¹⁶*And Jehovah God commanded the man, saying, Of every tree of the garden you may freely eat: ¹⁷but of the tree of the knowledge of good and evil, you shall not eat of it: for in the day that you eat thereof you shall surely die.*

The Hebrew word for "commanded," *tsavah*, is found here for the first time, and here is the first mention of an actual command in the Scriptures. The actual command includes a permission (v. 16b) and a prohibition (v. 17a). The purpose of the prohibition was the test of recognition of and submission to the will of God. Man was not to assume that because he was given authority over the earth, he was independent of God and exempt from God's law. As mentioned, man was created with the ability of contrary choice, and this was the moment when the parameters of his choice were set.

## C. Man's Probationary Period

In his state of innocence, man was on probation. During this time, he underwent a test whose object was two trees: *And out of the ground made Jehovah God to grow every tree that is pleasant to the sight, and good for food; the tree of life also in the midst of the garden, and the tree of the knowledge of good and evil* (Gen. 2:9). One tree in the midst of the Garden of Eden was *the tree of life*. Had Adam passed his probationary period, he would have been allowed to eat of the fruit of this tree and would have received eternal life without ever seeing death. The other tree was *the tree of the knowledge of good and evil*. Partaking of this tree meant that it would impart to Adam and Eve experiential knowledge (rather than head knowledge) of the difference between good and evil. If they disobeyed, Adam and Eve would know experientially—but also bitterly—what evil was and how it differed from good. Once they partook of this tree, they would have the power to do evil, but not the power to do the good that would commend them before God.

The nature of the test was simple: Man was allowed to partake of every other tree in the garden, except one. It is obvious that at the point of their testing, Adam and Eve had not partaken of the tree of life. They probably had no need to so early in their existence. Adam was given only one prohibitive commandment: *of the tree of the knowledge of good and evil, you shall not eat of it* (Gen. 2:17a).

It must be noted that the range of Adam's testing was quite limited in nature. Adam only had one possibility to fail: by repudiating God's will. Nowadays, man struggles with temptations such as covetousness or immorality. But Adam was lord of the earth, and he was married to the only woman around. Hence, covetousness and immorality were not issues for him. All he had to do was to obey God. There was no reason he should not have passed this test. The purpose of the test was to confirm his creaturely holiness.

The duration of the period of probation was temporary. After a period of time, there would have been a removal of the prohibition.

The goal of the probation was to confirm man's creaturely holiness so that he would pass from having the ability to sin to no longer having the ability to sin. If man had passed the test and resisted Satan's temptation, the probationary period would have ended. Consequently, man would have been put into a position of permanent sonship by means of the partaking of the tree of life.

## D. The Temptation

The main passage that details the temptation that brought about the fall of man is Genesis 3:1-6. Before looking at this passage, it must be noted that the exact time span between Genesis 2:25 and 3:1 is unknown. It is not known how long Adam and Eve were in the Garden of Eden before the temptation occurred.

The New Testament confirms that the event took place exactly as it is described in Genesis (e.g., Jn. 8:44; Rom. 5:12; 16:20; I Cor. 15:21; II Cor. 11:3-4; and I Tim. 2:14).

## 1. The Progression

The progression of man's first temptation is seen in Genesis 3:1-5:

> ¹*Now the serpent was more subtle than any beast of the field which Jehovah God had made. And he said unto the woman, Yea, has God said, Ye shall not eat of any tree of the garden?* ²*And the woman said unto the serpent, Of the fruit of the trees of the garden we may eat:* ³*but of the fruit of the tree which is in the midst of the garden, God has said, Ye shall not eat of it, neither shall ye touch it, lest ye die.* ⁴*And the serpent said unto the woman, Ye shall not surely die:* ⁵*for God does know that in the day ye eat thereof, then your eyes shall be opened, and ye shall be as God, knowing good and evil.*

As one studies the progression of man's temptation, it becomes clear that there were three stages. The first stage was an appeal to innocent appetites, seen in the serpent's question to Eve in verse 1b: *Yea, has God said, Ye shall not eat of any tree of the garden?* There was nothing wrong with eating; eating is an innocent appetite. In fact, God told Adam that he could partake of any tree in the entire garden, except one.

The second stage in the progression was the introduction of doubt, as the serpent asked, "Did God really say such a thing?" Suddenly, there was doubt concerning God's Word.

In the third stage, this doubt was turned into a direct attack on God's Word, when the serpent said: *Ye shall not surely die* (v. 4b). In Genesis 2:17, God had declared that if Adam partook of this one tree, he would die. Now, in Genesis 3:4, there was a denial of what God had said and thus a direct attack on God's Word.

Indeed, this is the typical progression of any temptation. It begins as an appeal to an innocent appetite. There is a right way and a wrong way to satisfy such an appetite. Once one begins to think in wrong ways of satisfaction, he begins to doubt the Word of God, and eventually, that which one merely doubts leads to a clearcut denial. That was the progression of the first temptation, and it is the progression of any temptation man has gone through ever since.

## 2. The Areas of Temptation

According to I John 2:14-16, there are three areas of temptation:

> ¹⁴*I have written unto you, fathers, because ye know him who is from the beginning. I have written unto you, young men, because ye are strong, and the word of God abides in you, and ye have overcome the evil one.* ¹⁵*Love not the world, neither the things that are in the world. If any man love the world, the love of the Father is not in him.* ¹⁶*For all that is in the world, the lust of the flesh and the lust of the eyes and the vainglory of life, is not of the Father, but is of the world.*

The three areas of temptation are the lust of the flesh, the lust of the eyes, and the pride of life. Man's first temptation touched on all three of these areas, as Genesis 3:6 shows: *And when the woman saw that the tree was good for food, and that it was a delight to the eyes, and that the tree was to be desired to make one wise, she took of the fruit thereof, and did eat; and she gave also unto her husband with her, and he did eat.*

In the area of the lust of the flesh, the woman saw that the tree was *good for food*. If she had been hungry, there were a lot of trees in the Garden of Eden, and she could have gone to any one of them to satisfy her hunger. That tree was good for food, but so were the other trees. Suddenly, the lust of the flesh came into the picture, and Eve felt she could only satisfy it with this particular fruit, and no other.

In the area of the lust of the eyes, the tree was *a delight to the eyes*. Before the temptation, Eve may never have noticed this tree as being more beautiful than any other. In fact, it probably was not more beautiful, but suddenly, that which was prohibited became the most beautiful.

In the area of the pride of life, *the tree was to be desired to make one wise*. There were other ways of gaining wisdom, but Eve now wanted to gain a special wisdom. She wanted to know good and evil. She wanted to be like God. This is the desire that caused the fall of Satan, who said in Isaiah 14:14b: *I will make myself like the Most High*. Eve now expressed the same desire; she wanted to be like God, knowing good and evil.

It is important to note that Adam was fully aware of what was going on. He was not away working. He was *with* his wife (Gen. 3:6). Yet, the Bible points out that there was a clear distinction between his fall and the fall of Eve. Twice it is stated that Eve was deceived. In I Timothy 2:14, Paul noted: *and Adam was not beguiled, but the woman being beguiled has fallen into transgression*. In II Corinthians 11:3, the apostle added: *But I fear, lest by any means, as the serpent beguiled Eve in his craftiness, your minds should be corrupted from the simplicity and the purity that is toward Messiah*. While Eve was deceived, Adam sinned with full knowledge, and by doing so, he committed an act of rebellion. Moreover, the Bible clearly places the responsibility for the human condition upon Adam as the representative head (Rom. 5:12-21, I Cor. 15:20-23). When he fell, he became guilty of breaking the Edenic Covenant, as Hosea 6:7 points out: *But they like Adam have transgressed the covenant: there have they dealt treacherously against me*.

## 3. The Creation of Wrong Desires

Man's first temptation created wrong desires. Three things can be mentioned about these desires. First, the temptation that brought on the fall of man created a desire to have what God had forbidden (Gen. 3:1-3). God had forbidden that Adam and Eve eat the fruit of this particular tree, but now they desired it.

Second, the temptation created a desire to be what God had not intended for man to be (Gen. 3:4-5). God did not intend for man to be like Himself; He made man human, not divine.

Third, this temptation created a desire to know what God did not reveal (Gen. 3:6). It promised the gaining of hidden knowledge and consequently led to the first delving of man into the occult world. Occult practices of any form are an attempt to go beyond the five senses in order to gain unrevealed or hidden knowledge.[57] Occultism makes promises of extra power, such as mental powers, miracles, and the ability to control people. Demons and occultism go hand in hand. In fact, occultism would not exist without demons. It always involves some contact with the demonic world, and Genesis 3:1-6 is the first example in the Scriptures of this truth. In this case, it was the prince of demons, Satan himself, who orchestrated the temptation and promised extra mental power to Eve.

## E. The Reason for Such a Great Penalty

When Adam gave in to the temptation, the consequences were dire. But why such a great penalty for such a simple sin of disobeying one command? Four points can be made in answer to this question. First, the command was indeed simple, but it was a test of the spirit of obedience. If man could not obey God in a slight command, how could he be trusted to obey a much greater command?

Second, the external command was not arbitrary or insignificant, but a concrete presentation to the human will of God's claim to His domain and absolute ownership. The command was a test to see if the will of man would submit itself to God's lordship.

Third, the sanction that was attached to the command shows that man was not left in ignorance of its meaning or importance. Man did not fail because of ignorance. He knew exactly what the command was and also what the consequences of violating this particular command would be. So, the sanction attached to the command shows that man was not left in ignorance of its meaning or importance.

Fourth, the act of disobedience was a revelation of a will alienated from God and corrupted. It was a will given to rebellion. Because the

---

[57] For a detailed analysis of what the Bible teaches about occultism, see: Arnold G. Fruchtenbaum, *A Study of the Angelic Realm: Angelology, Satanology, and Demonology* (San Antonio, TX: Ariel Ministries, 2020), pp. 127-133.

act of disobedience revealed a corrupted, rebellious will that was alienated from God, the punishment and the penalty were severe.

# F. The Fall

The fall of man itself will be discussed in four sections: the biblical record, self-justification, the consequences, and the dispensational consequences.

## 1. The Biblical Record

The fall of man is a crucial part of both the Hebrew Scriptures and the New Testament. It is impossible to remove the account and have the Bible make any sense at all. For example, Job 15:14 states: *What is man, that he should be clean? And he that is born of a woman, that he should be righteous?* Without the account of the fall, this verse does not make any sense.

The same is true for the following passages:
- Job 20:4-5: *⁴Know you not this of old time, Since man was placed upon earth, ⁵That the triumphing of the wicked is short, And the joy of the godless but for a moment?*
- Job 31:33: *If like Adam I have covered my transgressions, By hiding mine iniquity in my bosom;*
- Ecclesiastes 7:29: *Behold, this only have I found: that God made man upright; but they have sought out many inventions.*
- Romans 5:12-21: *¹²Therefore, as through one man sin entered into the world, and death through sin; and so death passed unto all men, for that all sinned:—¹³for until the law sin was in the world; but sin is not imputed when there is no law. ¹⁴Nevertheless death reigned from Adam until Moses, even over them that had not sinned after the likeness of Adam's transgression, who is a figure of him that was to come. ¹⁵But not as the trespass, so also is the free gift. For if by the trespass of the one the many died, much more did the grace of God, and the gift by the grace*

*of the one man, Yeshua Messiah, abound unto the many. [16]And not as through one that sinned, so is the gift: for the judgment came of one unto condemnation, but the free gift came of many trespasses unto justification. [17]For if, by the trespass of the one, death reigned through the one; much more shall they that receive the abundance of grace and of the gift of righteousness reign in life through the one, even Yeshua Messiah. [18]So then as through one trespass the judgment came unto all men to condemnation; even so through one act of righteousness the free gift came unto all men to justification of life. [19]For as through the one man's disobedience the many were made sinners, even so through the obedience of the one shall the many be made righteous. [20]And the law came in besides, that the trespass might abound; but where sin abounded, grace did abound more exceedingly: [21]that, as sin reigned in death, even so might grace reign through righteousness unto eternal life through Yeshua Messiah our Lord.*

- I Corinthians 15:21-22: *[21]For since by man came death, by man came also the resurrection of the dead. [22]For as in Adam all die, so also in Messiah shall all be made alive.*
- II Corinthians 11:3: *But I fear, lest by any means, as the serpent beguiled Eve in his craftiness, your minds should be corrupted from the simplicity and the purity that is toward Messiah.*
- I Timothy 2:13-15: *[13]For Adam was first formed, then Eve; [14]and Adam was not beguiled, but the woman being beguiled has fallen into transgression: [15]but she shall be saved through her childbearing, if they continue in faith and love and sanctification with sobriety.*

These examples clearly show that even when one goes beyond the Genesis record, the fall of man is very much an integral part of the biblical record in both the Hebrew Scriptures and the New Testament. So much of what happens in the Scriptures is based upon the fact of the fall. The ministry of Yeshua, for example, makes sense only in light of this event. Hence, to dismiss Genesis 3 as a myth is to contradict

Yeshua Himself (Mt. 19:5) as well as Luke (Lk. 3:23-38) and Paul (Acts 17:24-26; Rom. 5:12). They all viewed these events as historical, and they viewed Adam as a historical person. They knew the difference between truth and myth (I Tim. 1:4; 4:7; II Pet. 1:16).

## 2. The Self-Justification

The second thing to note about the fall of man is the procedure that Adam and Eve used to justify their actions. Eve's self-justification is implied in Genesis 3:6, where she made three points. First, she saw that the tree was good for food and said, "This is good food, and there is no reason why I should not eat it." Second, because the tree was a delight to the eyes, it had aesthetic value. So, she said, "Why should we not enjoy the beauties of life?" Third, the tree promised to make one wise. Therefore, Eve said, "What is wrong with wanting more wisdom?" In these three ways, Eve justified her eating, and that act of eating was an act of disobedience.

Adam, too, attempted to justify his actions. When God confronted him with his sin, he said in Genesis 3:12b: *The woman whom you gave to be with me, she gave me of the tree, and I did eat.* Adam did not make a simple confession, as he should have. He began his self-justification by blaming God indirectly ("The woman *you* put here with me..."). Then he blamed Eve directly ("She gave me some fruit from the tree."). His self-justification was based on the rationalization that a criminal becomes the victim. It shows how quickly sin had corrupted him. His admission of guilt came only at the end of the sentence, as he apparently wished to minimize, as much as possible, his own involvement in the sin.

## 3. The Immediate Consequences

The fall of man resulted in spiritual death, seen in its immediate consequences: i.e., a sense of guilt and shame, the desire to hide from God, judgment, and expulsion.

As to the sense of guilt and shame, this immediate consequence is described in Genesis 3:7: *And the eyes of them both were opened, and they knew that they were naked; and they sewed fig-leaves together, and made themselves aprons*. When the eyes of Adam and Eve were opened, they came to a certain understanding. However, it was not what the serpent had led them to believe. Rather, all of a sudden, Adam and Eve knew that they were naked. They had been naked all along, but suddenly there was a recognition of a new relationship between them. Their nakedness before each other created self-consciousness. What was once a sign of a healthy relationship in Genesis 2:25 had now become a sign of shame. There was the loss of innocence and the birth of lust. Instead of knowing good and evil in a positive sense, Adam and Eve now had an experiential knowledge of evil. The knowledge they gained was overwhelming, and they tried to hide their nakedness behind fig leaves. There was a recognition that the very source of human life had been contaminated by sin. Now the means by which the sin nature would be transmitted would be through the sexual union, because that is how children are conceived, as Psalm 51:5 shows: *in sin did my mother conceive me* Adam and Eve succeeded in hiding their nakedness from each other, but they did not succeed in hiding themselves from God. So now, nakedness before someone other than one's mate has become shameful, a shamefulness brought out in Genesis 9:23, Exodus 20:26, and Revelation 3:18.

Genesis 3:8 shows that another immediate consequence of the fall was the desire and effort to hide from God: *And they heard the voice of Jehovah God walking in the garden in the cool of the day: and the man and his wife hid themselves from the presence of Jehovah God amongst the trees of the garden*. Man's relationship with God changed with the fall. Adam and Eve had never tried to hide from God before, when God would regularly appear to them in some visible way in the cool of the day. Now, when they heard the voice of God, for the first time, there was a desire and an effort to hide from Him. The fellowship they used to have with God was no longer possible. There is a clear recognition of a new relationship with God, a negative one now. Therefore, there is guilt and there is fear of punishment; after hiding their nakedness from each other, they also tried to hide it from God. Their separation from God shows that they had died spiritually.

As to judgment, this immediate consequence came on four beings: the serpent (Gen. 3:14), Satan (Gen. 3:15), Eve (Gen. 3:16), and Adam (Gen. 3:17-19).

The last immediate consequence of the fall and the spiritual death that resulted from it was the expulsion from the Garden of Eden (Gen. 3:23-24).

### 4. The Dispensational Consequences

There were also certain dispensational consequences of the fall. The fall initiated a transition from the first dispensation, the Dispensation of Innocence, to the second dispensation, the Dispensation of Conscience.

Furthermore, the fall marked the termination of the Edenic Covenant and the inauguration of the second of the Bible's eight covenants: the Adamic Covenant.

## G. The Results

The fall had a negative impact on several of man's relationships. The first effect of the fall pertained to his relationship with God. It was at this point that the image of God in man was marred.

Second, man's relationship to his environment changed, in that the animal kingdom developed a strain of animals that became carnivorous. (Until the fall of man, all animals were vegetarians.) Furthermore, the material world and nature were cursed. Because of this curse, work became toilsome, and the land started to produce harshly. Man would have to battle thorns and thistles, droughts and floods (Gen. 3:17-18; 6:17-19).

Third, man's relationship with his body changed. Man became frail and was now subject to physical sickness, weakness, and illness, and ultimately even physical death.

Fourth, man's relationship with his nature changed in that he died spiritually. No longer did he live in a vital, living, spiritual relationship or fellowship with God. There are two aspects of spiritual death: total depravity and total inability. The first aspect, total depravity, can be defined both in terms of what it is not and what it is. Negatively, total depravity does not mean that man is as bad as he could be; he could be even worse. Total depravity does not mean that man is destitute of conscience or void of all good qualities. It does not imply that man commits every sin or that he is incapable of doing good. Positively, total depravity means that man is capable of every sin. He is devoid of love and obedience to God as demanded by the law of God. While man is not guilty of every sin, the point of total depravity is that sin extends to every part of man. Man is enslaved to sin and is dead in his trespasses. Sin has touched every part of his being (Jn. 5:42; 8:34; Rom. 7:23; Eph. 2:1; 4:18).

The second aspect of spiritual death is total inability. This means that man no longer has the power of contrary choice that he had before the fall. In his state of innocence, he was holy and perfect; he could choose to obey or disobey. But as a result of total depravity, there was now also total inability. Man no longer has the power of contrary choice. He can still choose, but only according to his nature, which is enslaved to sin and dead in trespasses. So, total inability means that the sinner cannot, by a single act or volition, bring his character and life into complete conformity with God's law. He cannot change his fundamental preference for sin in favor of the love of God. Man, in his natural, fallen state, is unable to respond to God. He cannot perform any act that will commend him to God (Jn. 6:44; Rom. 7:18; 8:7; I Cor. 2:14).

Fifth, the fall changed man's relationship with his guilt. Guilt means that there is an obligation to render satisfaction to God's justice, as determined by God's law. The very fact that man is declared to be guilty carries with it the obligation to render satisfaction to God's justice for the self-determined violation of God's law. Guilt is the objective result of sin (Rom. 1:18; 3:19; Eph. 2:3), and consequently, man deserves to be punished.

Sixth, the fall changed man's relationship to the penalty. The penalty means the pain or loss that is directly or indirectly inflicted by the lawgiver in vindication of his justice. This is the natural outworking of the declaration of guilt. For sin, the content of the penalty is death (Rom. 6:23). The penalty for the fall of man involved physical death, spiritual death, and eternal, or the second death. The only way that one can escape these penalties is to accept someone else's payment of the price. Yeshua, on the cross, took upon Himself the penalty of the Mosaic Law. If a person accepts the Messiah, then Yeshua has suffered the penalty in this person's stead, and the person will not have to pay the price. But, if one rejects the Messiah, then he will have to suffer this penalty.

## Chapter VII:
# The Biblical View of Death

The biblical view of death will be discussed in five sections: the origin of death, the meaning of death, death and the work of Messiah, death and the believer, and the abolishment of death.

## A. The Origin of Death

The Bible addresses three different types of death: spiritual death, physical death, and eternal death. In all three of its forms, death is viewed as being a result of the fall of man. Throughout the Scriptures, death is considered a penal evil (Gen. 2:16-17). The following passages are just some of the many examples that show this fact:
- Genesis 3:19: *In the sweat of your face shall you eat bread, till you return unto the ground; for out of it were you taken: for dust you are, and unto dust shall you return.*
- Ezekiel 18:4: *Behold, all souls are mine; as the soul of the father, so also the soul of the son is mine: the soul that sins, it shall die.*
- Romans 5:12: *Therefore, as through one man sin entered into the world, and death through sin; and so death passed unto all men, for that all sinned.*
- Romans 6:23: *For the wages of sin is death; but the free gift of God is eternal life in Messiah Yeshua our Lord.*
- I Corinthians 15:22: *For as in Adam all die, so also in Messiah shall all be made alive.*

So death originated with the fall and is a penal evil in that it is a penalty for sin.

## B. Definition

The best way of defining death, biblically speaking, is by the concept of separation. The term "separation" covers every usage of the word "death" in the Scriptures, both literal and symbolic. Anytime the word "death" is mentioned, separation is the best single meaning. Hence, death is not a cessation of existence nor a cessation of consciousness, but a separation.

The passage that best illustrates this definition is the account of the rich man and Lazarus (Lk. 16:19-31). This passage speaks of three people who are dead: the rich man, Lazarus, and Abraham. Yet, these three men carry on a conversation. They are very conscious and have feelings of pain and sorrow. This shows that death is not a cessation of existence or consciousness but a separation.

### 1. Physical Death

As mentioned, there are three types of death, the first of which is physical death. This type of death is the separation of the immaterial part of man from the material part of man, as Ecclesiastes 12:7 shows: *and the dust returns to the earth as it was, and the spirit returns unto God who gave it.* James 2:26 states: *For as the body apart from the spirit is dead, even so faith apart from works is dead.* Upon death, the material part of man separates from his immaterial part.

Until the fall of man, death was not part of the human experience, and the Scriptures make it very clear that physical death is a penalty for sin (Gen. 3:19; Num. 27:3; Ps. 90:7-10; Rom. 5:12-21; 6:23; I Cor. 15:21-22). Perhaps the best example of this truth is seen in Genesis 5, where the words "and he died" are recorded over and over again, with the exception of Enoch:

> [21]*And Enoch lived sixty and five years, and begat Methuselah:* [22]*and Enoch walked with God after he begat Methuselah three hundred years, and begat sons and daughters:* [23]*and all the days*

*of Enoch were three hundred sixty and five years: ²⁴and Enoch walked with God: and he was not; for God took him.*

Enoch did not die physically but went on to continually exist somewhere other than earth (Heb. 11:5).

For the believer, death is no longer viewed as a punishment, but rather as the means for entering into heaven. That is why the Bible describes death for the believer in terms of "sleeping" (Mk. 5:39; I Thess. 4:13-14). When the Bible uses the term "sleep" in reference to death it is not teaching soul-sleeping. This false view claims that upon death, the immaterial part of man goes into unconscious sleep and the person who dies remains unconscious in body and soul until the resurrection.

Seven arguments may be brought forth to disprove the doctrine of soul-sleeping. The first argument concerns the term "sleep" when it is used of death. Whenever the Bible speaks of death in the sense of sleep, it always does so in reference to the physical body and not in reference to the soul, because the appearance of a sleeping body and a dead body are very much the same. So, when the Bible speaks of sleep in the sense of death, it is only used of the body, not the soul. Furthermore, whenever the Bible uses the term "sleep" in reference to death, uniquely, it never does so in the context of unbelievers with one possible exception in Daniel 12:2. "Sleep" is a term used only of believers, which shows God's viewpoint of the death of a believer. From God's perspective, the death of a believer is a temporary suspension of physical activity. For example, in physical sleep there is a temporary suspension of physical activity until one wakes up. Yet, there is no suspension of the activity of the mind, the soul-spirit, and all the subconscious continues to operate. That is the way the Bible speaks of the believer whose physical activities are temporarily suspended upon death until the resurrection. But there is no suspension of soul-spirit activity.

The second argument against the teaching of soul-sleeping concerns consciousness after death. According to the Bible, a person is conscious after death (Mt. 17:1-8; Mk. 9:2-8; Lk. 9:28-36; 16:19-31).

The third argument against soul-sleeping pertains to the existence of angels, which proves that spirits can live and function apart from bodies. One of the reasons people teach that soul-sleeping must be true is because they believe that disembodied spirits cannot function. That is why some teach the existence of an intermediate body, and others teach soul-sleeping. However, the existence of angels shows that spirit beings can and do live and function apart from bodies (Heb. 1:14).

The fourth argument concerns the word "resurrection." This term applies only to bodies, never to souls. One will never read of a soul being resurrected from physical death (Mt. 27:52).

The fifth argument is based on the meaning of death. The clear teaching of Scripture is that upon death, the believer immediately enters into the presence of God (Acts 7:59; Phil. 1:23; II Cor. 5:6-8; Rev. 6:9-11; 7:9-17).

The sixth argument concerns the language of appearance. It pertains to passages that speak of the dead in terms of being in a state of unconsciousness. These passages are not dealing with the unconsciousness of the soul. Rather, being written in the language of appearance, they refer to the body. But the issue is not the body, the issue is the soul. The dead are unable to continue the processes that were normal for them when they were living on the earth, since their bodies can no longer function.

The seventh argument against the teaching of soul-sleeping concerns the determination of destiny. The destiny determined at the final judgment pertains only to the degree of punishment and not to the fact of punishment, present or future. There is present suffering for the soul of the unbeliever, with the worst to come after the final judgment. Now in hell, only the soul is suffering, but later in the lake of fire, there will be suffering of both the soul and the body. The verses that are used to try to prove that final determination is made only at the final judgment, not at death, too often confuse the two types of punishment. Again, the issue of salvation is determined upon death; the final judgment determines only the degree of punishment.

In summary, soul-sleeping is not the teaching of the Word of God, and for the believer, death is no longer a punishment; it is the means of entering into heaven. For the believer, therefore, it is viewed as "sleep," a temporary suspension of physical activity until the body awakens in the resurrection. The remedy for physical death is the resurrection of the body (Rom. 5:17; 8:23; I Cor. 15:22).

## 2. Spiritual Death

The meaning of spiritual death is separation from God (Mt. 8:22; Jn. 5:24; 8:51; Eph. 2:1, 5; 5:14; I Tim. 5:6; Jas. 5:20). Like physical death, spiritual death is also a penalty for sin. This is seen in Genesis 2:17, where God warned Adam that, on the day that he disobeyed the commandment, he would surely die. Obviously, Adam did not die physically the day he sinned, but he did die spiritually. When Adam and Eve sinned, they died toward God. Their nature became contrary to God's nature because it was now a fallen nature. It could no longer share the same level of fellowship with God that it had before the fall. As a result, all of Adam's descendants were born spiritually dead.

The natural man is spiritually dead, as I Corinthians 2:14 shows: *Now the natural man receives not the things of the Spirit of God: for they are foolishness unto him; and he cannot know them, because they are spiritually judged.* The natural man may not feel spiritually dead. He may not feel separated from God, but he is. Just like a physical corpse cannot feel that it is dead, for it has no feeling, in the same way, the natural man may not feel separated from God, but he is.

The remedy for spiritual death is to be made alive or "to be quickened" by faith in the Messiah (Jn. 5:24; Eph. 2:5-6; Col. 2:13).

## 3. Eternal or Second Death

According to Revelation 20:14 and 21:8, eternal death (or the second death) means separation from God in eternity (Mt. 10:28; 25:41; II Thess. 1:9; Jude 13; Rev. 14:11). Eternal death is spiritual death made permanent. It is a result of not believing on the Messiah as one's Savior (Jn. 3:17-18; 8:24; Acts 4:12).

The place where the separated ones, those who will experience this second death, will be for eternity is the lake of fire. Revelation 20:14-15 states:

> [14]And death and Hades were cast into the lake of fire. This is the second death, even the lake of fire. [15]And if any was not found written in the book of life, he was cast into the lake of fire.

The resurrection of the unbeliever will soon give way to the second death in the lake of fire, which will be the eternal abode of the lost.

Evangelistic preaching is generally centered around the necessity of believing in order to achieve two things: first, to avoid spending eternity in hell; and second, to spend eternity in heaven. Neither point is biblically correct. Throughout the pages of the Hebrew Scriptures, both the righteous and the unrighteous were said to go to a place called *Sheol* in Hebrew and *Hades* in Greek. While in the Hebrew Scriptures certain sacrifices covered the sins of the saints, they did not remove them (Heb. 10:4). Only the death of the Messiah could do that. So, while the sacrificial system was sufficient to keep people from hell, it was not able to get them into heaven. All who died, both the righteous and unrighteous, went to Sheol. This place contained two compartments. A description is found in Luke 16:19-31:

> [19]Now there was a certain rich man, and he was clothed in purple and fine linen, faring sumptuously every day: [20]and a certain beggar named Lazarus was laid at his gate, full of sores, [21]and desiring to be fed with the <crumbs> that fell from the rich man's table; yea, even the dogs come and licked his sores. [22]And it came to pass, that the beggar died, and that he was carried away by the angels into Abraham's bosom: and the rich man also died, and was buried. [23]And in Hades he lifted up his eyes, being in torments, and sees Abraham afar off, and Lazarus in his bosom. [24]And he cried and said, Father Abraham, have mercy on me, and send Lazarus, that he may dip the tip of his finger in water, and

*cool my tongue; for I am in anguish in this flame. ²⁵But Abraham said, Son, remember that you in your lifetime received your good things, and Lazarus in like manner evil things: but now here he is comforted and you are in anguish. ²⁶And besides all this, between us and you there is a great gulf fixed, that they that would pass from hence to you may not be able, and that none may cross over from thence to us. ²⁷And he said, I pray you therefore, father, that you would send him to my father's house; ²⁸for I have five brethren; that he may testify unto them, lest they also come into this place of torment. ²⁹But Abraham said, They have Moses and the prophets; let them hear them. ³⁰And he said, Nay, father Abraham: but if one go to them from the dead, they will repent. ³¹And he said unto him, If they hear not Moses and the prophets, neither will they be persuaded, if one rise from the dead.*

According to this passage, Hades (or Sheol) had two compartments. One was for the unrighteous, and it could be called "hell" in the way that term is used today; it was indeed a place of torment (vv. 23-25, 28). The other compartment, where the righteous went, was known as "Abraham's bosom" (v. 22); it was a place of comfort (v. 25), but it was not heaven. Elsewhere, the righteous portion of Sheol is called "paradise," since that is where the souls/spirits of believers were, as Luke 23:43 shows: *And he said unto him, Verily I say unto you, Today shall you be with me in paradise.*

While the people on the two sides could see each other and communicate with each other, they were separated by an immense gulf (v. 26) that made it impossible for someone on one side to cross over to the other side. In the Hebrew Scriptures, when a believer died, his body was buried in the earth while his soul went to Abraham's bosom, or paradise. When a sinner died, his body was also buried in the ground, but his soul went into hell.

When Yeshua died, He not only paid the price of all future sins, but also of all previous sins (Rom. 3:25; Heb. 9:15). Thus, the sins of the saints of the Hebrew Scriptures were removed. What happened next is described in Ephesians 4:8-10:

> ⁸*Wherefore he says, When he ascended on high, he led captivity captive, And gave gifts unto men. ⁹(Now this, He ascended, what is it but that he also descended into the lower parts of the earth? ¹⁰He that descended is the same also that ascended far above all the heavens, that he might fill all things.)*

While the body of Yeshua remained in the tomb, His soul went down into the paradise side of Sheol, announcing that the atonement had been made. At the time of His ascension, all the souls of the saints were removed from Abraham's bosom and brought into heaven. In this way, the righteous portion of Sheol was emptied and is no longer occupied.

Today, when an unbeliever dies, his body is still buried in the ground and his soul still goes into hell. However, when the believer dies, though his body is also buried in the ground, his soul goes immediately into heaven, as Paul revealed in II Corinthians 5:8: *We are of good courage, I say, and are willing rather to be absent from the body, and to be at home with the Lord.* To be in heaven at death is to be with the Messiah. Philippians 1:23 makes the same point: *But I am in a strait betwixt the two, having the desire to depart and be with Messiah; for it is very far better.*

## C. Death and the Work of the Messiah

Regarding the death and work of the Messiah, two things need to be discussed: the two types of resurrection and the kind of death Yeshua died.

### 1. The Two Types of Resurrection

When the Bible speaks of the resurrection from the dead, it distinguishes between two types of resurrection. The first type is a restoration back to natural physical life. A person who has undergone this type of resurrection will die again physically. In the Hebrew Scriptures, this restoration-type resurrection occurred twice: Elisha raised the

Shunammite's son back to life (II Kg. 4:32-37), and a man was suddenly resurrected from the dead when his corpse touched the bones of Elisha the prophet (II Kg. 13:20-21). In the New Testament, restoration-type resurrection occurred at least four times, in the cases of the daughter of Jairus (Mt. 9:18-26; Mk. 5:21-24, 35-43; Lk. 8:40-42, 49-56), of the son of the widow of Nain (Lk. 7:11-17), of Lazarus (Jn. 11:1-44), and of many saints the moment Yeshua died (Mt. 27:52-53). All of these resurrections were restorations back to natural physical life, and those who experienced them died again later.

The second type of resurrection from the dead leads to resurrection life, in which one is no longer subject to death. Paul made this point in Romans 6:9: *knowing that Messiah being raised from the dead dies no more; death no more has dominion over him*. True resurrection life means that a person is no longer capable of dying physically because there was a change in the nature of the body that has been resurrected. So far, Yeshua is the only One who has undergone this type of resurrection. Therefore, Paul called Him "the Firstfruits of the resurrection" in I Corinthians 15:23: *But each in his own order: Messiah the first-fruits; then they that are Messiah's, at his coming*. Colossians 1:15, 18 and Revelation 1:5 make the same point. Some have argued that this statement is contradictory, because how could Yeshua be referred to as "the Firstfruits of the resurrection" when others had been resurrected before Him? This question shows a failure to understand the two types of resurrection described in the Scriptures. All the others who were resurrected before Yeshua underwent the first type of resurrection, which was merely a restoration to natural life. Yeshua is the only One who has undergone the second type of resurrection that has led to true resurrection-life, so He is no longer subject to death.

Perhaps the best way to explain the means of true resurrection-life in contrast to restoration-life is by looking at Yeshua's example as a passing through death. Revelation 1:17-18 shows what this means:

*[17]And when I saw him, I fell at his feet as one dead. And he laid his right hand upon me, saying, Fear not; I am the first and the*

*last, ¹⁸and the Living one; and I was dead, and behold, I am alive for evermore, and I have the keys of death and of Hades.*

In these verses, Yeshua describes Himself as the Resurrected One. In the first type of resurrection, the resurrection back to natural life, one enters from the realm of physical life into the realm of physical death and then back into the realm of physical life. Yet, Yeshua did not merely come "out of" death. He passed through death, and that is the key. He went from the realm of physical life to the realm of physical death, and then He passed through death into the realm of resurrection-life.

Hebrews 2:14 also makes this point: *Since then the children are sharers in flesh and blood, he also himself in like manner partook of the same; that through death he might bring to nought him that had the power of death, that is, the devil.* The Greek word for "partook," *metechó*, means "to share in," "participate in." It could be translated as "being in the middle of something" or "taking hold of something that is not natural to one's nature." It is not natural for God's nature to have flesh and blood, but the Son added flesh and blood to His divine nature. Therefore, He could die and, by means of His death, render Satan's power inoperative. The Greek term for "bring to nought," *katargeó*, means "to render inoperative." The same word is used concerning the Mosaic Law (II Cor. 3:11-14). The Mosaic Law was not destroyed, but it was rendered inoperative. As a result, it no longer has legal authority over the believer. Throughout the history of the Hebrew Bible, Satan had authority over the physical death of both believers and unbelievers. This authority was his weapon against humanity. Today, Satan still has that authority over the deaths of unbelievers, but not of believers. His power in that realm has been rendered inoperative, and the Messiah took this weapon away from Satan. Messiah's counter-weapon is eternal life, which He obtained through His death.

Coming out of death is the first type of resurrection, while passing through death leads to the second type of resurrection, that of true resurrection-life (see Diagram A and B).

**Diagram A: Restoration-type Resurrection**

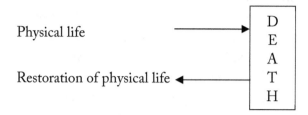

**Diagram B: Passing through Death — Resurrection Leading to True Resurrection Life**

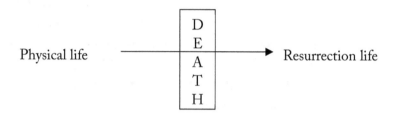

## 2. The Different Types of Death Suffered by the Messiah

The Messiah died two types of death: spiritual death and physical death. His spiritual death occurred during the second three hours of His crucifixion, when the entire world was enveloped in darkness (Mt. 27:45-50; Mk. 15:33-37; Lk. 23:44-46; Jn. 19:28-30). During these three hours of darkness, when the sins of the world were placed upon the Son, God the Father turned away. There was a separation between the Father and the Son, and for three hours, Yeshua the God-Man was spiritually dead. It must be emphasized that this was a separation in His humanity, not in His deity. When the Son of God took on the form of man at His incarnation, He was only one person, but with two distinct natures: a divine nature and a human nature. As for His divine nature, there was never any separation from the Father; that is, there was always an unending, uninterrupted fellowship with

God the Father. However, as for His human nature, there was a three-hour separation as Yeshua died spiritually on the cross.

At the end of these three hours, He cried: *Eli, Eli, lama sabachthani? That is, My God, my God, why have you forsaken me?* (Mt. 27:46b). Yeshua was quoting Psalm 22:1, which, along with Isaiah 53, contains the most detailed prophecy of Messiah's death. Taken in isolation, it might imply that Yeshua uttered a cry of despair and defeat. However, in the context of Psalm 22, Yeshua actually cried for help at the end of the three hours of His suffering the wrath of God. He died spiritually and was resurrected spiritually before finally dying physically on that cross. This is evident in the way He addressed God the Father. Here, He called Him "My God," and this was the only time in all four Gospels that He addressed God this way. Usually, He called Him "Father" (170 times) and, more intimately, "My Father" (21 times). Now, however, the relationship between the Father and the Son became judicial, and Yeshua did not address the Father as *Avi, Avi* ("My Father, My Father"), but *Eli, Eli* ("My God, My God"). His cry for help was answered in Luke 23:46, as He again called God His Father.

In summary, Yeshua died spiritually (Mt. 27:45-46; Mk. 15:33-34; Lk. 23:44) and was resurrected spiritually before He died physically (Mt. 27:50; Mk. 15:37; Lk. 23:46; Jn. 19:30). While His spiritual death allowed Him to become a sympathetic high priest (Heb. 2:17-18), His physical death was necessary for the atonement. Because of the types of death that Yeshua experienced on the cross, He changed the nature of death for the believer.

## D. Death and the Believer

The topic of death and the believer will be covered in four specific areas: how Messiah conquered death for the believer, how He causes death for the believer, how He consecrated death for the believer, and suicide.

## 1. The Messiah Conquered Death for the Believer

Yeshua the Messiah conquered death for the believer. According to Hebrews 2:9, He tasted death for all people: *But we behold him who has been made a little lower than the angels, even Yeshua, because of the suffering of death crowned with glory and honor, that by the grace of God he should taste of death for every man.* According to Hebrews 2:14-15, Messiah passed through death into resurrection-life. By doing so, He was able to conquer death after tasting death for every man.

When the Messiah went through death, He gained victory over death (Rev. 1:18). This means that Satan is no longer the lord of death for the believer. As mentioned before, throughout the history of the Hebrew Bible, the intertestamental period, and into the Gospel history until the death of Yeshua, it was Satan who was lord of death for all, believers and unbelievers alike (Job 1–2). But when Yeshua passed through death and gained victory over death, He took away the keys of death from Satan, so that the enemy is no longer the lord of death as far as believers are concerned (Gal. 1:4; Col. 1:13).

## 2. The Messiah Causes Death for the Believer

As far as believers are concerned, Yeshua the Messiah causes their death. The main passage that develops this truth is I Thessalonians 4:14: *For if we believe that Yeshua died and rose again, even so them also that are fallen asleep in Yeshua will God bring with him.* A more literal translation of the Greek text would be: "The believer has fallen asleep through Yeshua." The key word is "through." Again, when the Bible uses the term "sleep" in relation to death, it is not teaching soul sleeping but physical sleeping, in that it is the physical body that sleeps during death, not the immaterial part of man, the soul-spirit. Furthermore, whenever the Bible uses the term "sleep" in reference to death, it only uses it to speak of believers, never of unbelievers (with the possible exception of Dan. 12:2). When believers die, it is the Messiah who has put them to sleep as a means of bringing them home to be with Him.

Again, Satan still has the same power of death over the unbeliever as he did until Yeshua died on the cross, but he does not have the same power over the believer. There is one exception to this rule, and that is the case of an excommunicated believer. This is a believer who has undergone church discipline and has failed to respond to the four stages of Matthew 18:15-20 and, therefore, has been excommunicated. Excommunication means that the believer is placed back under the authority of Satan as far as his physical life is concerned. Satan then has the power to destroy the flesh. The passage that teaches about the excommunication of the believer is I Corinthians 5:1-5:

> *$^1$It is actually reported that there is fornication among you, and such fornication as is not even among the Gentiles, that one of you has his father's wife. $^2$And ye are puffed up, and did not rather mourn, that he that had done this deed might be taken away from among you. $^3$For I verily, being absent in body but present in spirit, have already as though I were present judged him that has so wrought this thing, $^4$in the name of our Lord Yeshua, ye being gathered together, and my spirit, with the power of our Lord Yeshua, $^5$to deliver such a one unto Satan for the destruction of the flesh, that the spirit may be saved in the day of the Lord Yeshua.*

When a believer is excommunicated, it means that he has committed the sin unto death mentioned in I John 5:16-17:

> *$^{16}$If any man see his brother sinning a sin not unto death, he shall ask, and God will give him life for them that sin not unto death. There is a sin unto death: not concerning this do I say that he should make request. $^{17}$All unrighteousness is sin: and there is a sin not unto death.*

Satan can put an excommunicated believer to death. The spirit of this believer is still saved, but his physical life is killed by Satan. Except for excommunicated believers, it is no longer Satan who puts believers to death but Yeshua who puts them to sleep (Mt. 27:52; Jn. 11:11-14;

Acts 7:60; 13:36; I Cor. 15:6, 18, 20, 51; I Thess. 4:13-14; II Pet. 3:4). The word "sleep" in relation to death shows God's view of the death of a believer in that it is merely a temporary suspension of physical activity until the believer wakes up in the resurrection.

### 3. The Messiah Consecrated Death for the Believer

Yeshua the Messiah has consecrated death for the believer, meaning He has changed the content of death. This does not mean that death has become a blessing, for death is never a blessing (I Cor. 15:26). Death is a product of the fall and was never part of God's perfect plan for man. But death does contain a blessing in that, by means of death, the believer goes into the very presence of God (II Cor. 5:8; Phil. 1:23).

Again, the believer does not fall asleep in his soul, but only in his body, for his soul goes immediately into God's presence. According to Hebrews 9:27, it is still appointed unto men once to die, but death is simply not the same thing for believers. It has been consecrated as far as the believer is concerned.

So there is no need for a believer to be afraid. When Yeshua died, He took away the fear of death from man (Heb. 2:14-15). The proper attitude a believer should therefore have regarding death is brought out in the following Scriptures:

- Psalm 116:15: *Precious in the sight of Jehovah Is the death of his saints.*
- II Corinthians 5:1: *For we know that if the earthly house of our tabernacle be dissolved, we have a building from God, a house not made with hands, eternal, in the heavens.*
- II Corinthians 5:6-8: *[6]Being therefore always of good courage, and knowing that, while we are at home in the body, we are absent from the Lord [7](for we walk by faith, not by sight); [8]we are of good courage, I say, and are willing rather to be absent from the body, and to be at home with the Lord.*
- Philippians 1:21-23: *[21]For to me to live is Messiah, and to die is gain. [22]But if to live in the flesh,—if this shall bring fruit from my*

*work, then what I shall choose I know not. ²³But I am in a strait betwixt the two, having the desire to depart and be with Messiah; for it is very far better.*

In II Timothy 4:6-8, Paul described his attitude toward his own approaching death:

*⁶For I am already being offered, and the time of my departure is come. ⁷I have fought the good fight, I have finished the course, I have kept the faith: ⁸henceforth there is laid up for me the crown of righteousness, which the Lord, the righteous judge, shall give to me at that day; and not to me only, but also to all them that have loved his appearing.*

All believers should follow Paul's example and develop this attitude toward death. They should recognize that their deaths will bring them into the very presence of God. For that reason, believers are not to be dismayed like the unbelievers who have no hope (I Thess. 4:13). There is a place for weeping for the loss of a loved one, as Yeshua wept over the death of Lazarus in John 11:35. There is a place for weeping and for sorrow, but not the type of sorrow that expresses hopelessness. Sorrow and tears, yes; lamenting and wailing, no.

## 4. Suicide

It has already been pointed out that Yeshua causes the deaths of believers. Does this include death by suicide? Before answering this question, it should be noted that Satan can use every type of death to kill an excommunicated believer. This includes death by suicide.

Regarding the other believers and the Messiah's role in their deaths, the Bible mentions six specific people who committed suicide: Abimelech (Judg. 9:54), Saul (I Sam. 31:4), Saul's armor-bearer (I Sam. 31:4-6), Ahithophel (II Sam. 17:23), Zimri (I Kgs. 16:18), and Judas (Mt. 27:5). Five of these men were noted for their wickedness. The exception is Saul's armor-bearer. Nothing is said about his character. Some consider Samson's death an instance of suicide because he knew his actions would lead to his death (Jdg. 16:26-31), but Samson's goal was to kill Philistines, not himself.

While the Bible records these suicides, it is silent on the theological implications of suicide. From the context of the biblical record of suicides, two things can be known: First, those who committed suicide were out of fellowship with the Lord; second, suicide is never the will of God. Suicide is an act of the human will over the divine will. It is not God's will for anyone, especially believers, to commit suicide. But one must be careful not to draw too many other theological and doctrinal conclusions from historical accounts.

The Messiah is the cause of death for believers if death is inflicted upon them or if they die naturally. Believers are capable of any and every sin when they are out of fellowship with the Lord, and one of these sins that they are capable of committing is the sin of suicide. Having said that, what is the spiritual status of the believer who committed suicide? Because of the silence of Scripture, we do not know all that we would like to know about this particular subject. But there are certain things that can be surmised.

It is very important to understand that suicide is not the unpardonable sin. The concept of suicide being the unpardonable sin originated with Roman Catholicism, which teaches that suicide is one of the seven deadly sins for which there can be no salvation. Unfortunately, many evangelical believers also hold this perspective and view suicide as an unpardonable sin that will send anyone to hell. However, the Bible teaches that that all believers are eternally secure (II Cor. 1:21-22; Eph. 1:13-14; 4:30). If this is true of all believers, then it is also true for the believer who commits suicide. The salvation of this person is assured, and the believer who has committed suicide is in the presence of the Lord.

Some believers object to this teaching by saying that suicide is a sin for which one does not have time to ask forgiveness. Therefore, that person cannot go to heaven. However, a believer's sin does not cause him to lose his salvation, and confession does not restore one to salvation. When a believer sins, he falls out of fellowship with God, but he does not "fall out" of his salvation. The purpose of confession is to restore fellowship (I Jn. 1:9), not to restore salvation. So, when a believer commits suicide, his salvation is still assured, because the Messiah died for all of his sins, not just some of them. The Messiah even died for the sin of suicide. Again, suicide is not the unpardonable sin. A person's salvation is assured. Even when a believer commits suicide, he still goes into the presence of God.

Furthermore, when a believer commits suicide, Romans 8:28 is still in effect. This verse states: *And we know that to them that love God all things work together for good, even to them that are called according to his purpose.* Just how things work out for the good of someone committing suicide may not be known in this life, but it will be understood in eternity.

As hard as it is to wrap one's mind around this truth, one has to realize that when a believer commits suicide, God allowed it. God can stop His children from committing suicide. He has even hindered unbelievers from doing so. Yet, at times, He chooses not to prevent the believer from committing this sinful act. For one reason or another, He allowed it. This, too, may not be understood in this life, but it will be in eternity.

Romans 8:1-2 stands for all believers, even those who are guilty of suicide:

> *¹There is therefore now no condemnation to them that are in Messiah Yeshua. ²For the law of the Spirit of life in Messiah Yeshua made me free from the law of sin and of death.*

At the Judgment Seat of the Messiah, there will be no condemnation for the believer who has committed suicide, because he was forgiven of all of his sins when he believed on the Messiah. There will certainly be a loss of rewards, but no condemnation.

Nothing said thus far changes the fact that the believer contemplating suicide must recognize the profound and long-term impact his decision will have on those left behind. The scars caused by suicide do not heal easily. God has commanded His children to love one another, and this love for one's neighbor includes thinking about the consequences of one's actions on others.

## E. The Abolishment of Death

Both spiritual and physical death can be abolished. As far as spiritual death is concerned, it is abolished at salvation according to II Timothy 1:10: *but has now been manifested by the appearing of our Saviour Messiah Yeshua, who abolished death, and brought life and immortality to light through the gospel*. Obviously, the Messiah has not as yet abolished physical death, for people still die physically. Yet, this verse speaks of a death that has been abolished for believers, and this death is connected with immortality. Hence, the death that has already been abolished for the believer is spiritual death. The moment one believes on Yeshua the Messiah—that He died for our sins, was buried, and rose again (I Cor. 15:4)—at that moment, the believer is spiritually resurrected, and spiritual death is abolished for him.

As far as physical death is concerned, a time will come when this, too, will be abolished. Paul stated in I Corinthians 15:24-26:

*²⁴Then comes the end, when he shall deliver up the kingdom to God, even the Father; when he shall have abolished all rule and all authority and power. ²⁵For he must reign, till he has put all his enemies under his feet. ²⁶The last enemy that shall be abolished is death.*

Some people think that Satan is man's final enemy and that once Satan is confined to the lake of fire, all problems will go away. However, as Paul pointed out, man's last enemy is not Satan, but that which entered human experience because of the Satanic temptation of the first parents: physical death. As a result of Adam's fall, death has been a cruel and relentless part of the human experience. Except for Enoch and Elijah, every human being in history has succumbed to it. A day will come when physical death is going to be abolished for believers and unbelievers alike, but there will be two different destinies altogether.

## 1. The Abolishment of Physical Death for the Believer

Concerning believers, one must distinguish between four different groups of believers: Old Testament saints, church saints, tribulation saints, and millennial saints.

### a. Old Testament Saints

Some time after the tribulation and the Messiah's second coming, death will be abolished for the saints of the Hebrew Bible. According to Daniel 12:11-12, there will be a seventy-five-day interval between the second coming and the start of the millennium. During this interval, the Old Testament saints are going to be resurrected.

This is brought out in Isaiah 26:19: *Your dead shall live; my dead bodies shall arise. Awake and sing, ye that dwell in the dust; for your dew is as the dew of herbs, and the earth shall cast forth the dead.* Here, Isaiah spoke of the resurrection of Old Testament saints, and the context shows that this resurrection will come after the tribulation. Daniel 12:2 makes the same point: *And many of them that sleep in the dust of the earth shall awake, some to everlasting life, and some to shame and everlasting contempt.*

### b. The Church Saints

As far as New Testament saints are concerned, physical death will be abolished for them at the rapture of the church. This is taught by two passages of Scripture.

The first passage is I Corinthians 15:50-58:

> [50]*Now this I say, brethren, that flesh and blood cannot inherit the kingdom of God; neither does corruption inherit incorruption.*[51]*Behold, I tell you a mystery: We all shall not sleep, but we shall all be changed,* [52]*in a moment, in the twinkling of an eye, at the last trump: for the trumpet shall sound, and the dead shall be*

*raised incorruptible, and we shall be changed. ⁵³For this corruptible must put on incorruption, and this mortal must put on immortality. ⁵⁴But when this corruptible shall have put on incorruption, and this mortal shall have put on immortality, then shall come to pass the saying that is written, Death is swallowed up in victory. ⁵⁵O death, where is your victory? O death, where is your sting? ⁵⁶The sting of death is sin; and the power of sin is the law: ⁵⁷but thanks be to God, who gives us the victory through our Lord Yeshua Messiah. ⁵⁸Wherefore, my beloved brethren, be ye stedfast, unmoveable, always abounding in the work of the Lord, forasmuch as ye know that your labor is not vain in the Lord.*

According to this passage, the believer's physical death will be abolished at the time of the rapture. At that point, corruption will put on incorruption, and mortality will put on immortality.

The second passage is I Thessalonians 4:13-18:

*¹³But we would not have you ignorant, brethren, concerning them that fall asleep; that ye sorrow not, even as the rest, who have no hope. ¹⁴For if we believe that Yeshua died and rose again, even so them also that are fallen asleep in Yeshua will God bring with him. ¹⁵For this we say unto you by the word of the Lord, that we that are alive, that are left unto the coming of the Lord, shall in no wise precede them that are fallen asleep. ¹⁶For the Lord himself shall descend from heaven, with a shout, with the voice of the archangel, and with the trump of God: and the dead in Messiah shall rise first; ¹⁷then we that are alive, that are left, shall together with them be caught up in the clouds, to meet the Lord in the air: and so shall we ever be with the Lord. ¹⁸Wherefore comfort one another with these words.*

Again, Paul pointed out that physical death would be abolished for the church saints at the rapture. This will occur some time before the tribulation.

### c. The Tribulation Saints

Tribulation saints will also be resurrected after the tribulation and during that seventy-five-day interval mentioned before. This is brought out in Revelation 20:4-6:

> *[4]And I saw thrones, and they sat upon them, and judgment was given unto them: and I saw the souls of them that had been beheaded for the testimony of Yeshua, and for the word of God, and such as worshipped not the beast, neither his image, and received not the mark upon their forehead and upon their hand; and they lived, and reigned with Messiah a thousand years. [5]The rest of the dead lived not until the thousand years should be finished. This is the first resurrection. [6]Blessed and holy is he that has part in the first resurrection: over these the second death has no power; but they shall be priests of God and of Messiah, and shall reign with him a thousand years.*

This passage clearly describes the tribulation saints, who refused to worship the Antichrist. Their resurrection occurs also in the seventy-five-day interval between the tribulation and the Messianic kingdom.

### d. The Millennial Saints

Millennial saints will not need to be resurrected because, according to Isaiah 65:20, they will not die: *There shall be no more thence an infant of days, nor an old man that hath not filled his days; for the child shall die a hundred years old, and the sinner being a hundred years old shall be accursed*. There will be no death for believers in the Messianic kingdom, only for unbelievers.

## 2. The Abolishment of Physical Death for the Unbeliever

For the unbeliever, physical death will be abolished after the Messianic kingdom. The abolishment will be a result of the resurrection of the unbelievers for the purpose of suffering the second death. This resurrection is the second resurrection described in the Bible. The first resurrection involves only believers (Rev. 20:5-6) and comes in stages in an orderly progression (I Cor. 15:20-23). The second resurrection, that of the unbelievers, is described in Revelation 20:11-14:

> *[11]And I saw a great white throne, and him that sat upon it, from whose face the earth and the Heaven fled away; and there was found no place for them. [12]And I saw the dead, the great and the small, standing before the throne; and books were opened: and another book was opened, which is the book of life: and the dead were judged out of the things which were written in the books, according to their works. [13]And the sea gave up the dead that were in it; and death and Hades gave up the dead that were in them: and they were judged every man according to their works. [14]And death and Hades were cast into the lake of fire. This is the second death, even the lake of fire.*

All unbelievers will be resurrected after the Messianic kingdom, meaning one thousand years after the last resurrection of believers has taken place. At that time, death will be abolished for unbelievers. However, they will experience another type of death, another type of separation from God, as they will spend eternity in the lake of fire. This death, called "the second death" in the Scriptures, will last forever for them. It will never be abolished.

# F. Questions and Study Suggestions

**Fill In the Blanks 1:**
a.  The best one-word description of the concept of death is _____.
b.  For believers, physical death is not viewed as a _____, but it is the means whereby the believer enters into _____.
c.  The "remedy" for physical death is _____.

**Question 2:** What is spiritual death?

**Question 3:** Read Genesis 2:17. What happened to Adam and Eve on the day they disobeyed? Describe the results.

**Question 4:** What is the "remedy" for spiritual death?

**Question 5:** What is eternal death?

**Question 6:** Is there a "remedy" for someone who is already eternally dead? What is the place of eternal death?

**Question 7:** What are the two types of resurrection? Name one biblical person who has been resurrected in each way.

**Question 8:** What does I Corinthians 15:23 mean?

**Fill In the Blanks 2:**
a.  In Old Testament times and until the death of Yeshua, it was _____ who caused the death of both believers and unbelievers when _____ permitted it.
b.  On the cross, Yeshua _____ death for the believer so that _____ is no longer the lord of death and no longer has that hold over the believer.

c. Since the death of Yeshua, it is _____ who causes the death of _____. It is _____ who causes the death of _____.
d. What is the one exception in the case of a believer's death? _____
e. What biblical term expresses the death of a believer, but never an unbeliever? _____
f. For the believer, death is a blessing. *(True / False)* Explain your answer.
g. Believers should not have a _____ of death.
h. The death of the believer is something that God considers _____.
i. When is spiritual death abolished? _____
j. How do we know that spiritual death is *permanently* abolished for us? _____
k. Physical death is abolished by means of _____ _____ from the dead. Which type? _____
l. According to I Corinthians 15:26, death itself shall be the _____ enemy to be abolished or "put under His [the Lord's] feet." Read Revelation 20:14. What is done with death itself? _____

Man and Sin

# Chapter VIII:
# Free Agency

The expression "free agency" refers to man's ability to make choices. It is man's power to choose between motives in a self-determined manner and to direct his subsequent activities according to the motive thus chosen. The question arises whether this is a biblical view. Is man a free and responsible agent in charge of his own actions? Can he decide between opposites?

The basic truth is that man is indeed a free agent. Only free agents can be held accountable for their character and conduct. However, man is not free to change his moral state by an act of the will.

## A. Total Inability

The Bible views man as incapable of choosing contrary to his nature. This does not mean a loss of free agency, but that the freedom of choice is limited to one's nature.

This inability of man especially concerns the things of the Spirit, as I Corinthians 2:14 points out: *Now the natural man receives not the things of the Spirit of God: for they are foolishness unto him; and he cannot know them, because they are spiritually judged.*

However, the inability of man also concerns salvation. This is seen in John 6:44: *No man can come to me, except the Father that sent me draw him: and I will raise him up in the last day.* Romans 8:7 provides a reason for man's inability to choose salvation: *because the mind of the flesh is enmity against God; for it is not subject to the law of God, neither indeed can it be.*

In the context of the discussion of John 6:44, theologians tend to bring up the term "calling." The basic definition of this expression is "the summoning of the elect." It is a special call to which only the elect respond. In their response to faith, they receive their salvation. This concept is also found in Hebrews 9:15b, which states: *they that have been called may receive the promise of the eternal inheritance.* In Romans 9:11b, Paul noted: *We have not been saved by works, but by Him who calls us.* In Romans 9:24, he repeated this statement and added that this calling goes out to both Jews and Gentiles: *He called to salvation both Jews and Gentiles.* While there is a general call, a call that goes out to all to proclaim the gospel, there is a special call to which the individual believer responds. These verses show that God responds to man's inability to choose contrary to his nature by actively calling people to faith.

## B. Free Will

Man's will is not determined by any law of necessity. It is not independent, indifferent, or self-determined. Rather, it is always determined by the preceding state of mind.

Man is a free and responsible agent insofar as he is the author of his own actions. Nothing outside of himself determines his actions. He acts according to his own views, convictions, inclinations, feelings, and disposition. A man is free so long as his volition gives the conscious expression of his own mind. As a result, his actions are true reflections of who he is and represent or reveal what he is. Free agency is the power to decide according to one's character, and humanity does have free will, but that free will is limited by man's nature. Man can do nothing toward his salvation, not even believe.

Based on this truth, some teach that regeneration must precede faith, that man must become spiritually alive before he can believe. They teach that faith is not the cause of the new birth, but the consequence of it. In other words, first one is born again, and then he believes.

This teaching is based on the extreme view of what total depravity means: that man has nothing to do with his spiritual birth. Salvation occurs with or without man's consent. It does not matter whether one wants to be saved or not; he is forced to be saved. If a person believes, it is because God has quickened him. If a person fails to believe, it is because God has withheld that grace.

How do those who hold this view answer the question, "What must I do to be saved?" (Acts 16:30). Paul answered the question rather simply: "Believe in the Lord Yeshua Messiah and you shall be saved." (Acts 16:31). Those who hold to the extreme view of total depravity, on the other hand, answer the question this way: "Nothing. You cannot do anything. You are dead and totally unable to respond to God until you are regenerated. You have no part in salvation. God must do it all. You cannot exercise saving faith until later on." In summary, one really cannot be saved until God gives him the faith to be saved.

That is the extreme view of total depravity. If one adheres to what the text says, total depravity means that man, left to himself, will not seek God. Total depravity is true if man is left to himself. But if God works and enables him to exercise belief that will bring about regeneration, then that is a different issue.

Even spiritually dead people make choices in the spiritual realm. They are able to choose lesser sins from greater sins. Unbelievers are able to resist temptations that believers fall into. So yes, unbelievers are spiritually dead, but the Bible does not picture them as corpses. They are seen as dead in certain areas, but not all areas.

According to the Bible, sin has corrupted and touched every part of man, so that left to his own devices, he will never respond to anything spiritual. Left to himself, as Paul said in Romans 3:11, no one will search for God. That is why if anybody was going to be saved, God had to take the initiative.

In this context, the topic of foreknowledge may be brought up as well. Foreknowledge means that an event may not be free, but it is certain. Certainty and free agency are not inconsistent.

## C. Conclusion

The Bible clearly shows that God has providential control over all events. How does this truth square with the free agency of man? God has the authority and right to do anything consistent with His nature, and He has chosen to exercise that authority by including the responsible and relatively free actions of man (Philemon 14; Rev. 17:13-17). Because man is a free agent, he can be held accountable when he fails to act responsibly.

## D. Questions and Study Suggestions

*Question 1:* What power did man possess prior to the fall that he no longer has?

*Question 2:* What does total inability mean in regard to man's freedom of choice?

*Fill In the Blanks and Choose the Right Answer:*
a. The unsaved man has a spiritually _____ nature. Therefore, the unsaved man **(can't / won't)** choose God. The unsaved man **(can't / won't)** choose salvation. The unsaved man **(can't / won't)** choose to obey the law of God.
b. Man **(is / is not)** a free agent.
c. None but free agents can be _____ _____ for their character and conduct.
d. Man does not possess the ability to _____ his moral state by an _____.
e. Man's will is always determined by the preceding _____.
f. Because of the _____ state of man's mind, he will always choose to _____ God.

# Chapter IX:
# The Glorification of Man

The Bible teaches that God's purpose for man is to bring him into a state of glorification. This chapter will examine the glorification of man in four facets: the resurrection of the human body, the nature of the resurrected body, the state of glorification, and the restoration of man's authority.

## A. The Resurrection of the Human Body

It is the clear teaching of the Scriptures that the human body, which is subject to death, will be resurrected. In the Hebrew Bible, this is taught in Job 19:25 27:

> [25]*But as for me I know that my Redeemer lives, And at last he will stand up upon the earth:* [26]*And after my skin, even this body, is destroyed, Then without my flesh shall I see God;* [27]*Whom I, even I, shall see, on my side, And mine eyes shall behold, and not as a stranger. My heart is consumed within me.*

Job had faith that, after his death, he would have a resurrected body and would be able to see God.

Another passage that teaches the resurrection of the human body is Daniel 12:2: *And many of them that sleep in the dust of the earth shall awake, some to everlasting life, and some to shame and everlasting contempt.* This verse speaks of the resurrection of all people. The unrighteous ones are destined for a place of shame and everlasting contempt. However, the righteous ones have a different destiny that has to do with their future glorification.

A third place where this truth is taught in the Hebrew Bible is Hosea 13:14: *I will ransom them from the power of Sheol; I will redeem them from death: O death, where are your plagues? O Sheol, where is your destruction? repentance shall be hid from my eyes.*

In the New Testament, the resurrection of the human body is taught in John 5:26-29:

> *²⁶For as the Father has life in himself, even so gave he to the Son also to have life in himself: ²⁷and he gave him authority to execute judgment, because he is a son of man. ²⁸Marvel not at this: for the hour comes, in which all that are in the tombs shall hear his voice, ²⁹and shall come forth; they that have done good, unto the resurrection of life; and they that have done evil, unto the resurrection of judgment.*

In this passage, Yeshua mentioned the resurrection of both the unrighteous and the righteous. The unrighteous ones are destined for the resurrection of judgment, but the righteous ones are destined for the resurrection of life and therefore their glorification.

The Apostle Paul mentioned the resurrection of the human body in I Corinthians 15:22-26 and stated that the abolition of death means resurrection:

> *²²For as in Adam all die, so also in Messiah shall all be made alive. ²³But each in his own order: Messiah the firstfruits; then they that are Messiah's, at his coming. ²⁴Then comes the end, when he shall deliver up the kingdom to God, even the Father; when he shall have abolished all rule and all authority and power. ²⁵For he must reign, till he has put all his enemies under his feet. ²⁶The last enemy that shall be abolished is death.*

In verses 51-53 of the same chapter, Paul mentioned a resurrection that leads to immortality:

> *⁵¹Behold, I tell you a mystery: We all shall not sleep, but we shall all be changed, ⁵²in a moment, in the twinkling of an eye, at the last trump: for the trumpet shall sound, and the dead shall be raised incorruptible, and we shall be changed. ⁵³For this*

*corruptible must put on incorruption, and this mortal must put on immortality.*

As Paul continued his discussion in verses 54-57, he quoted the previously mentioned passage in Hosea:

*⁵⁴But when this corruptible shall have put on incorruption, and this mortal shall have put on immortality, then shall come to pass the saying that is written, Death is swallowed up in victory. ⁵⁵O death, where is your victory? O death, where is your sting? ⁵⁶The sting of death is sin; and the power of sin is the law: ⁵⁷but thanks be to God, who gives us the victory through our Lord Yeshua Messiah.*

All of these passages emphasize the first truth concerning the glorification of man: the resurrection of the human body.

## B. The Nature of the Resurrected Body

The second facet of the glorification of man concerns the nature of the resurrected body. Ten things concerning this facet can be pointed out. First, as I Corinthians 15:35-44 shows, the resurrected body will be a spiritual body:

*³⁵But some one will say, How are the dead raised? and with what manner of body do they come? ³⁶You foolish one, that which you yourself sow is not quickened except it die: ³⁷and that which you sow, you sow not the body that shall be, but a bare grain, it may chance of wheat, or of some other kind; ³⁸but God gives it a body even as it pleased him, and to each seed a body of its own. ³⁹All flesh is not the same flesh: but there is one flesh of men, and another flesh of beasts, and another flesh of birds, and another of fishes. ⁴⁰There are also celestial bodies, and bodies terrestrial: but the glory of the celestial is one, and the glory of the terrestrial is another. ⁴¹There is one glory of the sun, and another glory of the moon, and another glory of the stars; for one star differs from another star in glory. ⁴²So also is the resurrection of the dead. It is sown in corruption; it is raised in incorruption: ⁴³it is sown in dishonor; it is raised in glory: it is sown in weakness; it is raised in power: ⁴⁴it is sown a natural body; it is raised a spiritual body. If there is a natural body, there is also a spiritual body.*

In this passage, Paul used certain terms in a figurative way. For example, when he mentioned the sowing of grain, he was referring to burials. When he spoke of sleeping, he was referring to death. Paul pointed out that the body that has been sown in burial and is sleeping in death will be resurrected. When the resurrection occurs, it means that the body will go from corruption to incorruption, from dishonor to glory, from weakness to power, from natural to spiritual.

The second thing concerning the nature of the resurrected body is that there will be a change in the body itself. The resurrection will not only lead to a change of residency, but also to a different body. The resurrected body will not be brand new in the sense of being completely unrelated to the old body. It will be a new body in the sense that the old body will be renewed from corruption to incorruption, from dishonor to glory, from weakness to power, and from natural to spiritual. The change will be in the nature of the body itself. Only the Messiah suffered no bodily corruption. This was predicted of Him in Psalm 16:10 and fulfilled in Acts 2:25-31. Everyone else will suffer corruption upon death. Until the resurrection of the believers, only the Messiah has immortality (I Tim. 6:16).

Third, the resurrected body will possess life (I Cor. 15:50-58; I Thess. 4:15-17).

Fourth, it will be a faultless body (Jude 24).

Fifth, it will be without blemish (Eph. 5:27).

Sixth, it will be a body characterized by holiness (Col. 1:22).

Seventh, it will be blameless and free from any guilt (I Thess. 5:23).

Eighth, it will be a free body, meaning it will no longer be subject to the limitations of sin and the sin nature (Rom. 8:21).

Ninth, it will be conformed to the resurrected Messiah, meaning that it is going to be conformed to the image of the Son of God Himself (Rom. 8:29).

Tenth, it will resemble the resurrected body of the Messiah (I Jn. 3:2).

## C. The State of Glorification

The third facet of the glorification of man concerns the state of glorification itself. It is God's will that man reaches a state of glorification. This is taught by a number of Scriptures, such as Romans 5:2: *through whom also we have had our access by faith into this grace wherein we stand; and we rejoice in hope of the glory of God*. Believers have the grace to stand before the throne of God; but as they stand in this grace, they are also standing in the hope of being glorified in the future.

In Romans 8:30, Paul stated: *and whom he foreordained, them he also called: and whom he called, them he also justified: and whom he justified, them he also glorified*. Glorification is the final product of God's destiny for those whom He has chosen. Those He foreordained, He then called; those whom He called, He also justified; those who now believe have been justified; and those who have been justified are also destined to be glorified.

In Philippians 3:20-21, Paul noted:

> [20]*For our citizenship is in heaven; whence also we wait for a Saviour, the Lord Yeshua Messiah:* [21]*who shall fashion anew the body of our humiliation, that it may be conformed to the body of his glory, according to the working whereby he is able even to subject all things unto himself.*

Believers are destined to undergo a physical change. The change will be from the present body, which Paul called *the body of our humiliation*, to the body of glory. This body will share the glory of the resurrected body of the Messiah.

Paul also wrote in I Thessalonians 2:12: *to the end that ye should walk worthily of God, who calls you into his own kingdom and glory*. The apostle exhorted the believers of Thessalonica to walk consistently with their calling as saints. They are destined for two future things: first, to enter the Messianic kingdom; and second, to enter into glory and to be glorified.

In II Thessalonians 2:14, Paul stated: *whereunto he called you through our gospel, to the obtaining of the glory of our Lord Yeshua Messiah*. Those who have accepted the gospel are destined to obtain the same type of glory that is now being enjoyed by Yeshua the Messiah Himself.

In II Timothy 2:10, Paul confirmed what he had said so far about the glorification of man: *Therefore I endure all things for the elect's sake, that they also may obtain the salvation which is in Messiah Yeshua with eternal glory*. Paul was willing to suffer—not only as a servant of God, but also on behalf of other saints—because he knew that all believers are destined to be glorified. Knowing this, he was willing to suffer to the extent that he did.

Hebrews 2:10 states: *For it became him, for whom are all things, and through whom are all things, in bringing many sons unto glory, to make the author of their salvation perfect through sufferings*. The writer of the book of Hebrews pointed out that the reason Yeshua became a man was so He might bring many other sons of men to a state of glory. Glory is the destiny of all believers.

Another writer who spoke along these lines was Peter, who wrote in I Peter 5:10: *And the God of all grace, who called you unto his eternal glory in Messiah, after that ye have suffered a little while, shall himself perfect, establish, strengthen you*. After their suffering on this earth is over, believers are going to enter into a state of eternal glory in the Messiah.

Peter spoke of this hope again in II Peter 1:3: *seeing that his divine power has granted unto us all things that pertain unto life and godliness, through the knowledge of him that called us by his own glory and virtue*. Believers are to walk consistently in accordance with their calling as saints because they are destined for future glorification. The salvation process is not yet complete for the believer. He is totally saved in the sense that this glorification is certainly going to come to pass. However, salvation contains a past aspect, a present aspect, and a future aspect. The past aspect of salvation is justification. The moment one accepts Yeshua and believes, he is justified and declared righteous in the holy court of God. The present aspect of salvation is sanctification. The work of sanctification is the work of the Holy Spirit who is setting apart the believer and conforming him more and more into the image of the Son of God. The future aspect of salvation is glorification. The believer will be glorified and will share in the glory of the resurrected Messiah—initially upon death and ultimately in the resurrection of the body.

## D. The Restoration of Man's Authority

The fourth facet that concerns the glorification of man is that man's authority is going to be restored. This point is made in Hebrews 2:6-8:

> *⁶But one has somewhere testified, saying, What is man, that you are mindful of him? Or the son of man, that you visits him? ⁷You made him a little lower than the angels; You crowned him with glory and honor, And did set him over the works of your hands: ⁸You did put all things in subjection under his feet. For in that he subjected all things unto him, he left nothing that is not subject to him. But now we see not yet all things subjected to him.*

When God created Adam and Eve, He gave man dominion over the earth. But when man fell to Satan's temptations, Satan usurped the authority over the earth from man. Rightfully and legally, from the viewpoint of divine law, the right to rule the earth was given to man, and he still has it. Yet, Satan stole the dominion from man. That is why he is called the prince of this world (Jn. 12:31) and the god of this age (II Cor. 4:4). One of the accomplishments of Messiah's second coming will be that the Ideal Man, the God-Man, Yeshua the Messiah will rule over this earth. Thus, dominion will be restored to man through the Messiah. When man once again gets to rule over this earth, something he has not been able to do since Adam's fall, then his authority will indeed be restored. This restoration will accomplish the final facet of man's glorification.

# Part 2:
# Hamartiology

# Chapter I:
# Introduction

Hamartiology is the doctrine of sin. It is the part of systematic theology that is concerned with the origins of sin and its impact on humanity. The Bible defines sin as missing the mark. A person who sins violates God's law (I Jn. 3:4) and rebels against Him (Deut. 9:7; Josh. 1:18). According to Romans 3:23, all have failed to meet God's standard of righteousness. Hamartiology explains why humans miss the mark, how they miss it, and what happens when they miss it.

Hamartiology is crucial for a proper understanding of God's plan of redemption. Before a person can comprehend salvation, he or she must first understand why salvation is even required. This is where hamartiology comes into play. It explains that all have sinned—by imputation, by inheritance, and by their own free will. It explains why God must judge each individual for his or her sins. Furthermore, hamartiology points to the solution to sin: the atoning sacrifice of Yeshua the Messiah.

There are eleven Hebrew words, seven Greek words, and ten English words that convey the concept of sin.

## A. Eleven Hebrew Words

The first and most common Hebrew root and term for "sin" is *chata*. This word is translated six different ways in the English Bible: "sin," "fault," "trespass," "harm," "blame," and "offense." The basic meaning of *chata* is "missing the mark." God intended for man to reach a certain goal. However, man has fallen short of this goal and has hit the wrong mark instead. Every departure from God's original plan is a falling short of the purpose for which man was created. Hence, sin is the missing of the goal that ought to be reached while hitting the wrong mark. Passages where this term is used include Genesis 4:7; 18:20; Exodus 32:30; and Leviticus 4:28.

The second Hebrew word is *pasha*, which is translated four different ways in the English Bible: "rebellion," "transgression," "sin," and "trespass." Its basic meaning is "to revolt" or "to refuse subjection to a rightful authority." The primary usage, sense, and meaning of this term are found in three passages, the first of which is I Kings 12:19: *So Israel rebelled against the house of David unto this day*. The second passage is Job 34:37: *For he adds rebellion unto his sin; He claps his hands among us, And multiplies his words against God*. The third passage is Isaiah 1:2: *Hear, O heavens, and give ear, O earth; for Jehovah has spoken: I have nourished and brought up children, and they have rebelled against me*. These passages utilize the primary meaning of *pasha*, which is "to revolt" or "to show a lack of subjection." From the primary meaning comes a derived meaning, which is seen in Psalm 51:13: *Then will I teach transgressors your ways; And sinners shall be converted unto you* (cf. Prov. 28:21; Isa. 43:27).

The third Hebrew word is *maal*, which is translated into English in three different ways: "trespass," "transgression," and "falsehood." This particular term points to the unfaithfulness or treachery of sin. It represents sin as a wrongdoing or a breach of trust. The term *maal* appears in passages such as Leviticus 5:15; Numbers 31:16; Joshua 7:1; and Ezra 9:2.

The fourth Hebrew word is *avah*, which is translated four different ways in the English Bible: "perversion," "wrong," "miss," and "iniquity." The basic meaning is "to be bent," "to be crooked," or "to be out of shape." It emphasizes the crookedness or distortion of sin. This meaning is found in Isaiah 21:3: *Therefore are my loins filled with anguish; pangs have taken hold upon me, as the pangs of a woman in travail: I am pained so that I cannot hear; I am dismayed so that I cannot see*. Another example is Lamentations 3:9: *He has walled up my ways with hewn stone; he has made my paths crooked*.

The fifth Hebrew word is *aven*, which is translated ten different ways in the English Bible: "vanity," "unjust," "unrighteous," "sorrow," "mourning," "affliction," "evil," "mischief," "wickedness," and "iniquity." The basic root meaning is "nothingness" and "a sense of nothingness." The term deals with a course of conduct that ultimately proves unprofitable to the doer. There is a stamp of nothingness and unreality on every departure from the law of God. The term emphasizes sin as being unreal in that it is not in conformity with the law of God. It presents the evil devices of men in their false, hollow, and unreal aspects. Because an idol was viewed by the prophets as a thing of naught, meaning as a vain and empty thing, this particular Hebrew word was often connected with the sin of idolatry. One example of this usage is Amos 5:5: *but seek not Beth-el, nor enter into Gilgal, and pass not to Beer-sheba: for Gilgal shall surely go into captivity, and Beth-el shall come to nought*. Another example is Isaiah 41:29: *Behold, all of them, their works are vanity and nought; their molten images are wind and confusion*.

The sixth Hebrew word is *rasha*, which is translated three different ways in the English Bible: "impiety," "wickedness," and "wicked one." Originally, the term emphasized the concept of activity. By connecting activity with sin, it emphasized the tossing and confusion in which the wicked live and the perpetual agitation that sinners cause others. This concept is seen in Job 3:17: *There the wicked cease from troubling; And there the weary are at rest*. Another example of the usage of *rasha* is Isaiah 57:20-21:

> [20]*But the wicked are like the troubled sea; for it cannot rest, and its waters cast up mire and dirt.* [21]*There is no peace, says my God, to the wicked.*

The seventh Hebrew word is *ra'*, which is translated a total of nineteen different ways in the English Bible:
1. Evil
2. Calamity
3. Distress
4. Adversity

5. Grief
6. Affliction
7. Misery
8. Sadness
9. Sorrow
10. Trouble
11. Sore
12. Noisome
13. Hurt
14. Heavy
15. Vex
16. Wretchedness
17. Harm
18. Ill
19. Mischief

The basic root meaning of this word is "to break up" or "to ruin." It binds together both the wicked deed and the consequences of that wicked deed. The term often refers specifically to the evil one whose sinful acts are an injury both to himself and to everyone around him. For the most part, this particular word implies that which is injurious rather than that which is a moral evil. It emphasizes the rough exterior of wrongdoing rather than the interior of morality. So, this word emphasizes sin as a breach of harmony or the breaking up of what is good and desirable in man's society. Some examples of the usage of *ra'* are Genesis 6:5; I Samuel 29:7; and Ezekiel 7:24.

The eighth Hebrew word is *amal*, which is translated six different ways in the English Bible: "travail," "toil," "trouble," "worrisome," "sorrow," and "pain." This particular term emphasizes the result of the first sin (the sin of Adam), which was toil in labor. Sin has made life a burden and has turned work into travail. Examples of the usage of *amal* are Genesis 41:51; Numbers 23:21; Deuteronomy 26:7; Judges 10:16; and Psalm 107:12.

The ninth Hebrew word is *avel*,[58] which is translated six different ways in the English Bible: "iniquity," "unjust," "unrighteousness," "ungodly," "perverse," and "wicked." The root meaning of this term is "a departure from that which is equal and right." *Avel* views and designates sin as the lack of integrity in wrongdoing. This concept is found in Malachi 2:6: *The law of truth was in his mouth, and unrighteousness was not found in his lips: he walked with me in peace and uprightness, and turned many away from iniquity.*

The tenth Hebrew word is *avar*, which is translated for the most part by one English word: "transgression." Transgression requires a specific boundary or border to cross over, and that boundary is a specific law or commandment of God. Once one has sinned, he has crossed over the boundary of right and entered into the forbidden land of wrong. This concept is found in Joshua 6:7: *And they said unto the people, Pass on, and compass the city, and let the armed men pass on before the ark of Jehovah.* An example of transgression in the sense of sin can be seen in Numbers 14:41: *And Moses said, Wherefore now do ye transgress the commandment of Jehovah, seeing it shall not prosper?*

The eleventh and final Hebrew word for "sin" is *asham*, which is translated two ways in the English Bible: "guilt" and "trespass." It emphasizes sin that is committed through error, negligence, or ignorance. The moment this type of sin comes to a person's knowledge, he is guilty and should regard himself as having offended. Perhaps the best picture of this term is the *asham* (or trespass) offering detailed in Leviticus 4:13-14, 22-23, 27-28; and 5:2-6.

## B. Seven Greek Words

The first of the seven Greek words that carry the concept of sin is *hamartia*. This term is the primary Greek word translated as "sin." Just as the corresponding Hebrew word *chata*, *hamartia* has the basic

---

[58] Also transliterated as *evel*, *avlah*, and *olah*.

meaning of "missing the mark." Conversely, to miss the mark means "to hit the wrong mark." This term, used in the sense of missing the mark, is found in Romans 3:23: *for all have sinned, and fall short of the glory of God*.

The second Greek word is *parabasis*, which is translated, for the most part, as "transgression." Romans 2:23 shows that the transgression implied is the breaking of the law: *you who glory in the law, through your transgression of the law dishonor you God?* Other examples are Romans 4:15 and Galatians 3:19.

The third Greek word is *adikia*, which is translated as "unrighteousness." It emphasizes the lack of righteousness that is characteristic for sin (e.g., Lk. 13:27; Jn. 7:18; Acts 8:23).

The fourth Greek word is *asebeia*, which is translated as "impiety." It emphasizes the lack of holiness that sin contains. This particular concept is found in I Timothy 1:9: *as knowing this, that law is not made for a righteous man, but for the lawless and unruly, for the ungodly and sinners, for the unholy and profane, for murderers of fathers and murderers of mothers, for manslayers*. Other examples are I Peter 4:18 and Jude 15.

The fifth Greek word is *anomia*, which carries the meaning "lawlessness." This term emphasizes sin as having contempt for the law. It also emphasizes sin as being in violation of the law. Therefore, it is sometimes translated as "iniquity." Sin is iniquitous. One example of this meaning is found in I John 3:4: *Every one that does sin does also lawlessness; and sin is lawlessness*.

The sixth Greek word is *ponēros*, which means "deprived," "evil," "wicked," and "bad." In passages such as Matthew 6:23, it emphasizes rapacity, which is the fruit of covetousness: *But if your eye be evil, your whole body shall be full of darkness. If therefore the light that is in you be darkness, how great is the darkness!*

The seventh Greek word is *epithumia*, meaning "desire," "lust," and "passionate longing." It emphasizes sin as a desire, particularly a desire or lust for that which is forbidden. An example of this usage is in I

Thessalonians 4:5: *not in the passion of lust, even as the Gentiles who know not God.*

## C. Ten English Words

To fully understand the biblical teaching concerning sin, one must consider ten specific English words. These words are based on the eleven Hebrew terms and seven Greek terms that were studied above.

The first English word is "transgression." Transgression emphasizes the overstepping of a boundary and the violation of a specific commandment. Hence, the term highlights a specific type of sin: a deliberate act that goes against a known commandment of God.

The second English word is "iniquity," which emphasizes that which is altogether wrong. Some things, by themselves, are neutral. They become wrong only in the way they are used. However, an iniquity is something that is altogether wrong. There is no correct or righteous way to use it.

The third English word, summarizing the biblical concept of sin, is "error." Sin is an error in the sense that it is a disregard for that which is right. It is an error in the sense of going astray.

The fourth English word is "sin." While all other expressions basically emphasize a specific type or concept of sin, this term should always be understood in its broader and general meaning. It describes a coming short or a falling short and is both a missing of the mark and a hitting of the wrong mark.

The fifth English word is "wickedness." Wickedness emphasizes the outworking and expression of the human will in its depraved state. When the human will works out its desire in its depravity, the result is wickedness.

The sixth English word is "evil," meaning "a wrong." Sin is wrong in that it is anything and everything that stands in opposition to God. What opposes God is a wrong, and what is wrong is sin.

The seventh English word is "ungodliness." This particular term emphasizes sin as lacking any fear of God. It is living a life of ungodliness with no concern that it may bring about divine discipline and judgment.

The eighth English word is "disobedience." This term emphasizes sin as the unwillingness to be led or guided in the way of truth as revealed by the Word of God. The disobedience spoken of here may be active disobedience (such as transgression) or it may be passive disobedience. It is always the result of an unwillingness to be led or guided in the way of truth as revealed by the Word of God.

The ninth English word is "unbelief," which emphasizes sin as being a lack of trust and faith in God. The Scriptures teach that *whatsoever is not of faith is sin* (Rom. 14:23). The specific type of sin that is not of faith is unbelief.

The tenth English word is "lawlessness," which emphasizes sin as going contrary and lacking conformity to the law. It is living a life of lawlessness, a life that does not see itself as being bound by divine law (I Jn. 3:4-10).

These ten English expressions help to define and summarize the Hebrew and Greek words for sin. They show that sin covers a wide spectrum. Sin is not merely a lack of something and cannot be defined purely by one particular aspect. In fact, many false concepts of sin are based upon seeing sin as covering only one aspect. For example, some view sin as nothing but a limitation of being holy. Others see sin as merely a lack of love. Some see sin as a desire for that which is wrong. Some see sin as a principle of evil. Some define sin as selfishness. Some see sin as an illusion. Some see sin as a violation of the law. While all of these concepts are involved in the biblical teaching of sin, by themselves, none of them adequately defines sin. Rather, they all must be considered in order to understand the full concept of sin.

## Chapter II:
# What Is Sin?

## A. Developing a Definition

In light of the various Hebrew, Greek, and English usages studied in the previous chapter, how is sin to be defined? Five specific elements need to be included in a definition of sin: First, sin is selfishness; second, sin is a transgression of known law; third, sin is a wrong attitude and a wrong desire of the will or the self; fourth, sin is unbelief; and fifth, sin is the voluntary disobedience of an explicit command of God.

A very simple definition that includes all five of these elements is this: **Sin is anything contrary to the character of God.**

This simple definition covers all five elements: Selfishness is contrary to the character of God; transgression of known law is contrary to the character of God; a wrong attitude and desire of self are contrary to God's character; unbelief goes contrary to God's character; and voluntary disobedience of an explicit command of God goes contrary to God's character. So the simple definition of sin as being anything contrary to the character of God covers all usages and concepts of sin in Scripture. Furthermore, it covers all eleven of the Hebrew words, the seven Greek words, and the ten English words.

A more detailed definition would be: **Sin is any lack or want of conformity to the character of God, whether it is an act, a disposition, or a state.**

## B. The Essential Nature of Sin

Having provided a definition of the term "sin," the essential nature of sin needs to be determined. Ten things should be noted here. First, sin is a specific type of evil.

Second, sin is a lack of conformity to or a transgression of the law of God. As James 4:17 shows, it is a failure to do what the law demands: *To him therefore that knows to do good, and does it not, to him it is sin*. As Paul noted in Galatians 3:10, to fail in one point of the law is to be guilty of breaking the whole law: *For as many as are of the works of the law are under a curse: for it is written, Cursed is every one who continues not in all things that are written in the book of the law, to do them* (cf. Jas. 2:10). Ignorance of the law is not an excuse. While it may lessen the degree of punishment, it does not lessen the duration of punishment. Yeshua made this point in Luke 12:47-48:

> [47]*And that servant, who knew his lord's will, and made not ready, nor did according to his will, shall be beaten with many stripes;* [48]*but he that knew not, and did things worthy of stripes, shall be beaten with few stripes. And to whomsoever much is given, of him shall much be required: and to whom they commit much, of him will they ask the more.*

The lack of the ability to obey is not the measure of obligation or test of what sin is. Sin is there, whether or not one feels he is able to keep the law. Nor is the feeling of guilt necessary for the fact of sin. Sin is present regardless of whether or not one feels guilty. Sin is any lack or want of conformity to or a transgression of the law of God.

Third, sin is a principle or a nature, as well as an act. This can be seen in Matthew 15:19: *For out of the heart come forth evil thoughts, murders, adulteries, fornications, thefts, false witness, railings* (cf. Jer. 17:9; Lk. 6:45). As an act, sin produces guilt. As a principle, sin produces pollution. Because sin is both a nature (or principle) and an act, it produces a sixfold result:

1. It darkens the understanding of man (Rom. 1:31; I Cor. 2:14; Eph. 4:18).

2. It produces an evil and vain imagination (Gen. 6:5, 12; Rom. 1:21).
3. It produces vile affections or passions (Rom. 1:26-27).
4. It produces corrupt speech (Eph. 4:29).
5. It produces a defiled mind and conscience (Titus 1:15).
6. It produces an enslaved and depraved will (Rom. 7:18-19).

Fourth, the essential nature of sin is selfishness. Ultimately, sin emphasizes the sinner himself as being primary, as opposed to the primacy of God.

Fifth, sin is also lawlessness (I Jn. 3:4) in that it contains the aspect of a failure to live in accordance with the law and commandants of God.

Sixth, sin has an absolute character. It is not some vague influence (Mt. 10:32-33; 12:30; Lk. 11:13; Jas. 2:10).

Seventh, sin always has a relationship with God and His will (Rom. 1:32; 2:12-14; 4:15; 5:13; Jas. 2:9-10).

Eighth, sin includes both guilt and pollution. Concerning guilt, it makes man liable for punishment (Rom. 3:19; 5:18; Eph. 2:3). Concerning pollution, all men are guilty of moral pollution in Adam because they are born of a corrupt nature. Moral pollution means that there is a disposition toward evil (Job 14:4; Is. 6:5; Jer. 17:9; Rom. 8:5-8; Eph. 4:17-19).

Ninth, sin has its roots in the heart. Sin influences the intellect, the emotion, and the will, and it finds expression through the body (Prov. 4:23; Jer. 17:9; Mat. 15:19-20; Lk. 6:45; Heb. 3:12).

Tenth, sin does not consist of outward acts only. There is a three-stage progression to sinful acts:
1. Sin consists of a sinful state (Mt. 5:22, 28).
2. The sinful state becomes the basis for sinful habits (Rom. 7:7).
3. These sinful habits result in sinful deeds (Rom. 7:17, 24).

**Chapter III:**

# The Origin and Universality of Sin

## A. Where and How Did Sin Begin, and Who it Its Author?

The Bible teaches in no uncertain terms that God cannot sin. According to I John 1:5, there is no darkness in Him: *And this is the message which we have heard from him and announce unto you, that God is light, and in him is no darkness at all.* God is incapable of sinning. He cannot even be tempted to sin: *Let no man say when he is tempted, I am tempted of God; for God cannot be tempted with evil, and he himself tempts no man* (Jas. 1:13). Being unable to sin, God did not create sin. Yet, sin was anticipated in His foreknowledge and was included in His plan. This is seen in the fact that the plan of God included a Savior from before the foundation of the world: *every one whose name has not been written from the foundation of the world in the book of life of the Lamb that has been slain* (Rev. 13:8b).

Although God is not the author of sin, He is the Creator of the one who is himself the author of sin. The closest the Bible comes to revealing the actual origin of sin is in relationship to Satan. Concerning Satan, Ezekiel 28:15 states: *You were perfect in your ways from the day that you were created, till unrighteousness was found in you.* At some point, Satan was found to have sinned. He was the first creature to sin. The nature of that first sin was Satan's desire to be like God. He said: *I will ascend above the heights of the clouds; I will make myself like the Most High* (Isa. 14:14). In John 8:44b, Yeshua called Satan the father of sin who did not abide in the truth: *He was a murderer from the beginning, and stands not in the truth, because there is no truth in* him. *When he speaks a lie, he speaks of his own: for he is a liar, and the father thereof.*

In summary, God is neither the originator nor the author of sin, but the Creator of the one who is the author of sin: Satan. Satan was the first sinner, and the first sin was pride, expressed in Satan's desire to be like God. This is the actual origin of sin.

The origin of sin in relation to angels is found in Revelation 12:3-4:

*³And there was seen another sign in heaven: and behold, a great red dragon, having seven heads and ten horns, and upon his heads seven diadems. ⁴And his tail draws the third part of the stars of heaven, and did cast them to the earth: and the dragon stands before the woman that is about to be delivered, that when she is delivered he may devour her child.*

According to this passage, one third of the angels participated in the satanic revolt against the authority of God and consequently fell into sin. Thus, sin originated with Satan. Then one third of the angelic host fell with him.

With man, sin began in the Garden of Eden with Adam's fall. Paul made this point in Romans 5:12, where he stated: *Therefore, as through one man sin entered into the world, and death through sin; and so death passed unto all men, for that all sinned.* The nature of the first human sin is the same as that of the first angelic sin: the desire to be like God. This can be seen in Genesis 3:5: *for God does know that in the day ye eat thereof, then your eyes shall be opened, and ye shall be as God, knowing good and evil.* The actual act of sin was disobedience to a specific commandment, as Genesis 2:16-17 shows:

*¹⁶And Jehovah God commanded the man, saying, Of every tree of the garden you may freely eat: ¹⁷but of the tree of the knowledge of good and evil, you shall not eat of it: for in the day that you eat thereof you shall surely die.*

This point is repeated in Genesis 3:6: *And when the woman saw that the tree was good for food, and that it was a delight to the eyes, and that the tree was to be desired to make one wise, she took of the fruit thereof, and did eat; and she gave also unto her husband with her, and he did eat.*

## B. Sin Is Universal

The Scriptures clearly teach that sin is universal. With the exception of Yeshua of Nazareth, all who are born of Adam and Eve are guilty of sin. This fact can be seen in two ways. First, there are clear, direct statements from both the Old and New Testaments showing that everyone is guilty of sin. The following are just a few examples of this truth:

- I Kings 8:46: *If they sin against you (for there is no man that sins not), and you be angry with them, and deliver them to the enemy, so that they carry them away captive unto the land of the enemy, far off or near.*
- Psalm 143:2: *And enter not into judgment with your servant; For in your sight no man living is righteous.*
- Proverbs 20:9: *Who can say, I have made my heart clean, I am pure from my sin?*
- Ecclesiastes 7:20: *Surely there is not a righteous man upon earth, that does good, and sins not.*
- Romans 3:9: *What then? are we better than they? No, in no wise: for we before laid to the charge both of Jews and Greeks, that they are all under sin.*
- Romans 3:19-23: [19]*Now we know that what things soever the law says, it speaks to them that are under the law; that every mouth may be stopped, and all the world may be brought under the judgment of God:* [20]*because by the works of the law shall no flesh be justified in his sight; for through the law comes the knowledge of sin.* [21]*But now apart from the law a righteousness of God has been manifested, being witnessed by the law and the prophets;* [2]*even the righteousness of God through faith in Yeshua Messiah unto all them that believe; for there is no distinction;* [23]*for all have sinned, and fall short of the glory of God;*

- Galatians 3:22: *But the scripture shut up all things under sin, that the promise by faith in Yeshua Messiah might be given to them that believe.*
- James 3:2: *For in many things we all stumble. If any stumbles not in word, the same is a perfect man, able to bridle the whole body also.*
- I John 1:8: *If we say that we have no sin, we deceive ourselves, and the truth is not in us.*

The second way to show the universality of sin is by pointing out three implications. The first implication is that, according to the Bible, man is a sinner from birth. This can be seen in passages such as the following:

- Job 14:4: *Who can bring a clean thing out of an unclean? not one.*
- Psalm 51:5: *Behold, I was brought forth in iniquity; And in sin did my mother conceive me.*
- John 3:6 *That which is born of the flesh is flesh; and that which is born of the Spirit is spirit.*

The second implication is that, according to the Bible, even infants are sinful. This can be seen in Romans 5:12-14:

> $^{12}$*Therefore, as through one man sin entered into the world, and death through sin; and so death passed unto all men, for that all sinned:—* $^{13}$*for until the law sin was in the world; but sin is not imputed when there is no law.* $^{14}$*Nevertheless death reigned from Adam until Moses, even over them that had not sinned after the likeness of Adam's transgression, who is a figure of him that was to come.*

The third and final implication is that all human beings, including children, are under condemnation, as Yeshua pointed out in John 3:3b: *Verily, verily, I say unto you, Except one be born anew, he cannot see the kingdom of God.* Paul made the same point in Ephesians 2:3: *among whom we also all once lived in the lusts of our flesh, doing the desires of the flesh and of the mind, and were by nature children of wrath, even as the rest.*

The result of the universality of sin is fivefold:
1. Human beings are subject to death in all of its forms: physical death, spiritual death, and eternal death.
2. They are born spiritually dead and in a state of depravity.
3. They are guilty of personal sins.
4. They are in a state of being under sin.
5. They are under the continuous influence of Satan.

**Chapter IV:**

# Man's Estate under Sin

All human beings live under sin. Paul made this point in Romans 3:9: *What then? are we better than they? No, in no wise: for we before laid to the charge both of Jews and Greeks, that they are all under sin.* He repeated this verdict in Romans 7:14b: *I am carnal, sold under sin.* In Galatians 3:22, he explained: *But the scripture shut up all things under sin, that the promise by faith in Yeshua Messiah might be given to them that believe.* According to the Scriptures, then, all human beings live in what the theologian Louis Sperry Chafer called "the estate under sin."[59]

## A. The Meaning of "Living under Sin"

In Romans 3:9, the Greek word for "under" is *hupo*. This preposition refers to the condition of man as being under the authority or dominion of someone or something that is outside of himself. All humans live in a system that holds dominion over them. This system is the result of a divine reckoning. By divine decree, all humans were placed under sin. They live in a system in which sin holds dominion over them. By divine decree, all Jews and Gentiles have been placed into that estate in which human merit is worthless as far as salvation is concerned. Every human merit is discarded to the end that the uncompromising, saving grace of God may be exercised on those who believe.

---

[59] Louis Sperry Chafer, *Major Bible Themes: 52 Vital Doctrines of the Scriptures Simplified and Explained* (Grand Rapids, MI: Zondervan, 1974), p. 180.

Living in an estate under sin puts unbelievers in a unique relationship with Satan. According to II Corinthians 4:3-4, Satan blinds their minds:

*³And even if our gospel is veiled, it is veiled in them that perish: ⁴in whom the god of this world has blinded the minds of the unbelieving, that the light of the gospel of the glory of Messiah, who is the image of God, should not dawn upon them.*

In Ephesians 2:1-2, Paul called unbelievers "the sons of disobedience" and explained Satan's control over them:

*¹And you did he make alive, when ye were dead through your trespasses and sins, ²wherein ye once walked according to the course of this world, according to the prince of the powers of the air, of the spirit that now works in the sons of disobedience;*

According to Colossians 1:13, being in the estate under sin means to live in Satan's kingdom of darkness: *who delivered us out of the power of darkness, and translated us into the kingdom of the Son of his love.*

According to I John 5:19, the world is in an estate under sin. Therefore, the whole world is under the control of the evil one: *We know that we are of God, and the whole world lies in the evil one.*

## B. The Remedy for Man's Estate

The remedy for man's estate under sin is not to stand on one's own merit, but to stand on the merit of the Messiah. Human merit simply has no value in salvation. Man cannot do anything to change his estate. Therefore, all human merit is to be discarded. Only when a person stands on the Messiah's merit will he or she change estates. Only then will they move out of the estate of being under sin and into the new estate of being under grace. Paul made this point in Romans 6:14: *For sin shall not have dominion over you: for ye are not under law, but under grace.*

# Chapter V:
# The Sin Nature — Original Sin

The passage that deals with the sin nature and man's original sin in depth is Romans 1:18–3:20. This division will be covered in five areas.

## A. The Meaning of Original Sin

The expression "original sin" has two different meanings and can be used in two ways. Sometimes the expression refers to the first sin committed by a human being, and Romans 5:19 reflects this meaning: *For as through the one man's disobedience the many were made sinners, even so through the obedience of the one shall the many be made righteous.* In this verse, "original sin" means that Adam's sin brought original guilt and original pollution. This original pollution caused total depravity and inability so that even man's best works are still radically defective in the eyes of a just and holy God. In summary, the expression "original sin" can refer to Adam's sin.

The second and more common usage of the phrase refers to the sin nature. The sin nature is called "original sin" because it originated with Adam and flows from the first parents (Adam and Eve) so that everyone inherits this nature. Chafer called this sin nature "Adamic nature."[60] Furthermore, the sin nature is sometimes called "original sin" because it is the origin of all other sins. All people commit acts of sin due to their sin nature.

A simple definition of the sin nature is this: The sin nature is the capacity to do all things, either good or bad, that in no way commend

---

[60] Chafer, *Major Bible Themes*, p. 178.

a person to God. All human beings enter life as sinners and commit acts of sin because they are sinners. Adam and Eve are the only two people who ever *became* sinners by sinning. All their descendants sin because they *are* sinners. Only Adam and Eve died spiritually by sinning. Their descendants are born spiritually dead. Because they are born with a sin nature, they commit acts of sin.

The sin nature is not an essential element of the immaterial part of man but a corruption of the very essence of the soul. Adam and Eve lived for a period of time without a sin nature. Yeshua existed all of His life without a sin nature. Again, the sin nature is the capacity to do both good and bad things that in no way commend a person to God.

In summary, every human being is born with original sin. How this Adamic nature is transmitted to them will be discussed under Point C. As will be seen, the sin nature remains an active force in the believer's life. It is not eradicated or removed in this life, but the believer has the power to overcome it by the indwelling Spirit (Rom. 8:4; Gal. 5:16-17).

## B. The Concept Taught in Scripture

The concept of the sin nature is taught throughout the Bible. In the Hebrew Scriptures, the sin nature is spoken of in the following passages: Genesis 6:5; 8:21; Job 15:14, 16; Psalm 58:1-3; 94:11; 130:3; 143:2; Ecclesiastes 7:20; 9:3; Isaiah 64:6; Jeremiah 13:23; 16:12; and 17:9. In the New Testament, the sin nature is spoken of in these verses: Matthew 7:11; 12:34; 15:19; Romans 6:20; I Corinthians 2:14; Ephesians 4:18; Colossians 2:13; I Peter 4:2; I John 1:8; and 2:16. These examples show that the Bible does indeed teach the concept of a sin nature and original sin.

## C. The Transmission of the Sin Nature

The sin nature is transmitted by what is called "mediate transmission." This means that the sin nature was transmitted from Adam to all of his descendants and from them through all the mediators of all the generations until this day.

It is important to understand that the sin nature does not come directly from Adam to each individual. Rather, it came from Adam through all of his descendants, through our parents, to us. Conversely, children inherit their sin nature from their parents, and parents from their parents, all the way back to Adam.

This point is made in Psalm 51:5: *Behold, I was brought forth in iniquity; And in sin did my mother conceive me.* In the New Testament, it is reiterated in Ephesians 2:3: *among whom we also all once lived in the lusts of our flesh, doing the desires of the flesh and of the mind, and were by nature children of wrath, even as the rest.*

## D. The Penalty for the Sin Nature

God judged the sin nature of man, and the penalty for the original sin involved two things: total depravity and spiritual death. By way of definition, total depravity does not mean that every person is as bad as he or she can be. Rather, total depravity refers to the unmeritorious state of man before God. None of man's works carries any merit before God. As far as spiritual death is concerned, all humans are born spiritually dead because they inherit the sin nature upon conception (Gen. 2:17; I Cor. 2:14; Eph. 2:1, 5).

God's penalties for the sin nature carry with them four specific results:

1. There is a corruption of the very nature of the soul in that the soul is rendered spiritually dead.
2. There is the loss of original righteousness. When Adam and Eve were created, they had original righteousness, but they lost it when they sinned. Now, the inclination of man is toward evil.
3. It is the nature of sin to include guilt and corruption. Guilt refers to the outward aspect of sin; corruption refers to the inward aspect of sin.

4. The sin nature retains its character even in believers. This is the reason believers still sin.

## E. The Remedy for the Sin Nature

The remedy for the sin nature involves three things, each of which has a different effect or result.

First, the remedy for the sin nature involves regeneration. To be regenerated means "to be born again." Hence, regeneration renders the dead spirit alive. The dead spirit, with which man is born, is quickened at the moment of belief. The result of regeneration is that the believer becomes spiritually alive.

Second, the remedy for the sin nature involves redemption. Redemption brings with it a new capacity to serve God with righteousness. Believers still retain their sin nature. However, as a result of redemption, they receive a new nature that allows them to serve God with righteousness.

Third, the remedy for the sin nature involves the indwelling presence of the Holy Spirit. The result is that believers can gain victory over the sin nature by the power of the Holy Spirit. Believers in Yeshua the Messiah are regenerated, redeemed, and indwelled by the Holy Spirit. The overall result is spiritual life.

Chapter VI:

# Personal Sin

Having studied the origin and effects of the sin nature as well as its remedy, the next topic is personal sin. One key verse that deals with the concept of personal sin is Romans 3:23, where Paul stated that *all have sinned, and fall short of the glory of God.*

## A. Definition and Classification

The expression "personal sin" refers to acts of sin committed by individuals. While the sin nature is inward, personal sin is outward; it is the act of sin. These acts of sin are committed because man is by nature a sinner. They may be willful acts, or they may be committed out of ignorance. Either way, they are still acts of sin. In summary, personal sin includes everything in daily life that is against God or fails to conform to the character of God.

Personal sin can be divided into various classifications:
- As related to divine requirements, personal sins could be those of commission or omission.
- As related to object, personal sins could be directed against God, against a neighbor, or against oneself.
- As related to compass or direction, personal sins could be inward (of the soul) or outward (of the body).
- As related to chargeability, personal sin could be chargeable to oneself alone or to others as partakers.
- As related to intention, personal sin could be voluntary or involuntary, which means that sinful acts can be committed out of ignorance or because of passion.

- As related to sinfulness, personal sins could come in greater and lesser degree, because the Bible does teach the concept of lesser and greater sins.
- As related to subject, personal sins are committed by the saved and unsaved, to the saved and unsaved, and against the saved and unsaved.
- As related to God's justice, personal sin could be dealt with by God either because of His vengeance or on the basis of His longsuffering.
- As related to forgiveness, personal sins are either forgiven or unforgiven.
- As related to cause, personal sins could be caused either by ignorance, impudence, malice, helplessness, or premeditation.
- As related to penalty, personal sins are partially judged in this world, or they will be judged in the world to come.

## B. The Concept Taught in Scripture

There are a number of Scriptures that teach the concept of personal sin. The following passages are just a few examples of a much wider body of text:

- According to I Kings 8:50a, personal sins are violations of God's law: *and forgive your people who have sinned against you, and all their transgressions wherein they have transgressed against you;*
- In Psalm 19:13a, personal sins can be presumptuous: *Keep back your servant also from presumptuous sins.*
- Psalm 51:4 teaches that personal sins are against God: *Against you, you only, have I sinned, And done that which is evil in your sight; That you mayest be justified when you speak, And be clear when you judge.*
- Psalm 90:8 speaks of secret sins that are personal sins: *You have set our iniquities before you, Our secret sins in the light of your countenance.*

- Luke 12:47-48a speaks of sins of both ignorance and of knowledge: *⁴⁷And that servant, who knew his lord's will, and made not ready, nor did according to his will, shall be beaten with many stripes; ⁴⁸ᵃbut he that knew not, and did things worthy of stripes, shall be beaten with few stripes.*
- Luke 15:21 teaches that personal sins are directed against heaven: *And the son said unto him, Father, I have sinned against heaven, and in your sight: I am no more worthy to be called your son.*
- Luke 23:34a teaches that personal sins can also be those of ignorance: *And Yeshua said, Father, forgive them; for they know not what they do* (cf. Acts 3:17-19; I Tim. 1:13).
- John 19:11 speaks of greater and lesser personal sins: *Yeshua answered him, You would have no power against me, except it were given you from above: therefore he that delivered me unto you has greater sin.*
- I Corinthians 6:9-10 speaks about sinful actions: *⁹Or know ye not that the unrighteous shall not inherit the kingdom of God? Be not deceived: neither fornicators, nor idolaters, nor adulterers, nor effeminate, nor abusers of themselves with men, ¹⁰nor thieves, nor covetous, nor drunkards, nor revilers, nor extortioners, shall inherit the kingdom of God* (cf. Gal. 5:19-21).

The Scriptures clearly teach that personal sins exist and that they arise out of man's sinful nature.

## C. The Transmission of Personal Sin

Personal sin originates from the sin nature. It is because human beings have a sin nature that they commit acts of sin. The sin nature is transmitted from Adam through the parents. It is inherited from one's parents upon conception, and then acts of sin are committed because of that sin nature.

The consequences of personal sin may affect one's descendants for four generations because, according to Exodus 34:6-7, the justice of

God sometimes requires that the sins of the fathers be visited *upon the children, and upon the children's children, upon the third and upon the fourth generation*. However, this principle only applied to Israel living under the Mosaic Law. It is not applicable to New Testament saints, and the Law of Messiah does not mention generational sins for church saints (meaning the body of the Messiah). When Messiah died, He died for all sins, and all sins are forgiven with regeneration.

## D. The Penalty for Personal Sin

The two facets concerning the penalty for personal sin are guilt and the degree of punishment. Because of personal sin, the unsaved sinner stands guilty before a righteous and holy God.

Furthermore, personal sins add to the degree of punishment. For believers, obedience leads to reward and greater responsibility. Those who are faithful in little things will be entrusted with much more, and the reward will be greater. The principle is: *to whomsoever much is given, of him shall much be required: and to whom they commit much, of him will they ask the more* (Lk. 12:48b). For the believer, this means different degrees of reward.

The reverse is also true. For the unbeliever, it means lesser or greater degrees of punishment: *that servant, who knew his lord's will, and made not ready, nor did according to his will, shall be beaten with many stripes; but he that knew not, and did things worthy of stripes, shall be beaten with few stripes* (Lk. 12:47-48a). Throughout Scripture, God repeatedly teaches that the degree of punishment will be based upon the degree of sinfulness of the unbeliever. These verses also show that the amount of knowledge will also be taken into consideration. Those to whom much knowledge about the gospel was given will receive a greater punishment than those who heard little. The punishment is proportionate to the opportunities missed, and in the verses above, both the servant who knew and the servant who did not know were beaten.

In summary, the Bible teaches that there will be degrees of punishment for unbelievers. The result of the penalty for personal sin will be a state of lostness. If one does not believe in Yeshua the Messiah in this life, he is lost forever.

## E. The Remedy for Personal Sin

Concerning the remedy for personal sin, there are two facets involved: forgiveness and justification. When individuals receive Yeshua as their Savior, they are forgiven of their sins. God removes the sins of those who have exercised faith in the substitutionary death, burial, and resurrection of the Messiah. The first penalty for personal sin—guilt—is removed by forgiveness.

The second facet of the remedy for personal sin is justification. To be justified means "to be declared righteous." The one who believes in Yeshua the Messiah is declared to be righteous. Justification also involves a declaration of non-guilt. The Messiah's righteousness is reckoned to the account of the believing sinners so that they are no longer at risk of being cast into the lake of fire for all eternity.

In summary, the result of the remedy for personal sin is personal salvation.

Man and Sin

# Chapter VII:
# Imputed Sin

## A. Definition

The word "impute" means "to reckon to one's account." It means attributing something to someone. The Bible speaks of three great imputations, the first of which is the imputation of Adam's sin to the human race. The second imputation is that of the sin of man to the Messiah; this occurred on the cross. The third imputation is the imputation of Messiah's righteousness to the believer; this happens when one believes. This study focuses only on the first great imputation, which is the foundation for the other two.

Adam's sin was imputed to the entire human race. All humankind is viewed as having participated in Adam's disobedience, and therefore, all humanity carries the same guilt. Every human being has a sin nature and is guilty of his or her own personal sins. But they are also guilty because they are viewed as having participated in Adam's sin.

The most effective way to illustrate this biblical truth is the concept of a power of attorney. When you appoint someone as your power of attorney, he or she has complete authority to act on your behalf. His actions on your behalf are interpreted as your own. If he commits an illegal act, you share responsibility, and to some extent, the attorney's guilt will be imputed to you because you granted him power of attorney. Adam was vested with the authority to act on behalf of the human race. As a result, when he sinned, the entire human race sinned.

From the biblical perspective, God sees all humanity as being "in Adam" (I Cor. 15:22). Thus, all humans are reckoned as being guilty, not only of their own sin, but also of Adam's sin.

## B. The Concept Taught in Scripture

The one key passage that teaches the concept of imputed sin is Romans 5:12-21. The key sentence in this passage is verse 12: *Therefore, as through one man sin entered into the world, and death through sin; and so death passed unto all men, for that all sinned.* In the way it is phrased, the "all" who sinned are viewed in connection with Adam's sin. It is through him that sin entered into the world, and death through sin. Death was passed on to all humans because all are considered to have sinned "in Adam." It is because of this imputation that even infants sometimes die, although they may not have had an opportunity to sin.

## C. The Transmission of Imputed Sin

Apart from the concept of the power of attorney, another way to explain how imputed sin is transmitted is by the theological term "natural headship." Adam was the progenitor of the entire human race. Through him, sin and death entered the world. Natural headship implies that Adam's sin is transmitted immediately or directly to the individual. Because humanity as a whole has a seminal relationship with Adam, it is viewed as having participated in his sin. In summary, according to the doctrine of natural headship, Adam's sin is transmitted immediately, or directly, to the individual.

It is important to distinguish between the transmission of the sin nature and the transmission of the imputed sin. The sin nature is passed on by mediate transmission. It originates with Adam, passes through the generations to one's parents, and finally reaches the individual. Imputed sin, on the other hand, is passed on by immediate transmission in that it goes from Adam directly to each individual member of the human race, not through the parents.

As a result of the organic unity of the human race in Adam, the sin of Adam is imputed and transmitted immediately to all of his descendants. This biblical concept is known as "seminal relationship." An illustration of such a relationship is seen in Hebrews 7:9-10:

> [9]*And, so to say, through Abraham even Levi, who received tithes, has paid tithes;* [10]*for he was yet in the loins of his father, when Melchizedek met him.*

The background to this passage is Genesis 14, where Abraham paid tithes to Melchizedek. The author of Hebrews points out that when Abraham paid tithes, Levi, who was a descendant of Abraham, was also viewed as having paid tithes to Melchizedek by means of imputation through a seminal relationship. Levi was not even born when that event occurred. Nevertheless, because he was *in the loins of his father*, Abraham, Levi was viewed as having paid tithes to Melchizedek.

The entire human race originated "in the loins of Adam." As a result of this seminal relationship, when Adam sinned, all humanity is viewed as having participated in the sin. Hence, Adam's sin is imputed to all humanity because it is also considered to be the sin of every individual since Adam. According to Romans 5:12, death passed to all men because they all sinned in Adam, who was the natural head of the human race by virtue of a seminal relationship.

In summary, the sin nature is transmitted through mediate transmission, as it originates with Adam and is passed on to us through our parents. Imputed sin is transmitted directly from Adam to us.

## D. The Penalty for Imputed Sin

According to Romans 5:12, the penalty for imputed sin is physical death. This was already taught in Genesis 3:19: *in the sweat of your face shall you eat bread, till you return unto the ground; for out of it were you taken: for dust you are, and unto dust shall you return.*

Other passages that teach the same truth are Romans 5:14 and I Corinthians 15:20-23.

## E. The Remedy for Imputed Sin

The remedy for imputed sin is the third great imputation that was mentioned previously: the imputed righteousness of the Messiah. This truth is taught in conjunction with the doctrine of imputed sin in the context of Romans 5:12-21. Verse 21 states: *that, as sin reigned in death, even so might grace reign through righteousness unto eternal life through Yeshua Messiah our Lord.*

Another passage that teaches that the remedy for imputed sin is the imputed righteousness of the Messiah is II Corinthians 5:21. The verse begins with the words: *Him who knew no sin he made to be sin on our behalf.* This statement is dealing with the second great imputation: the imputation of the sin of man upon the Messiah. The verse continues: *that we might become the righteousness of God in him.* The righteousness of the Messiah is imputed upon the believer.

This truth is also taught in I Corinthians 15:20-26, 54-56, with the key concept being spelled out in verse 22: *For as in Adam all die, so also in the Messiah shall all be made alive.*

# Chapter VIII:
# Sin in the Believer's Life

Believers do commit acts of sin. In this regard, the sin in the believer's life is comparable to personal sin committed by unbelievers. These acts of personal sin committed by individual believers may be deliberate or unintentional. They may be willful acts of sin or acts done out of ignorance.

## A. The Concept Taught in Scripture

Scripture makes it abundantly clear that believers continue to commit acts of sin. In I Timothy 1:15, Paul referred to himself as the chief of sinners: *Faithful is the saying, and worthy of all acceptation, that Messiah Yeshua came into the world to save sinners; of whom I am chief.* Paul was an apostle, and he may have attained the epitome of spirituality that man can achieve in this life. Yet, when he wrote his letter to Timothy at the end of his life, he did not use the past tense. He did not say, "I used to be the chief of sinners." Rather, he expressed himself in the present tense: "I *am* chief." He continued to regard himself as a sinner by nature and saw himself as committing acts of sin.

Another significant passage that speaks about sin in the believer's life is I John 1:8-10:

> [8]*If we say that we have no sin, we deceive ourselves, and the truth is not in us.* [9]*If we confess our sins, he is faithful and righteous to forgive us our sins, and to cleanse us from all unrighteousness.* [10]*If we say that we have not sinned, we make him a liar, and his word is not in us.*

John addressed his epistle to believers. In verse 8, he emphasized that believers retain their sin nature. In verse 9, he mentioned that believers commit specific acts of sins that must be confessed. In verse 10, he addressed the issue of personal sins, stating that if believers claim that they have not sinned, they expose themselves as liars. Take note of John's use of the personal pronoun "we" in this verse. He included himself in this statement. Hence, according to Scripture, believers do commit personal acts of sin, and there is sin in the believer's life.

## B. The Relationship to Other Categories of Sin

What is the relationship between sin in the believer's life and man's estate under sin, the sin nature, personal sin, and imputed sin?

When it comes to man's estate under sin, believers are no longer living in that estate; rather, they now reside in the new estate of being "under grace."

In terms of the sin nature, believers retain their sin nature. Just as the sin nature is the source of personal sins committed by unbelievers, the sin nature is also the source of personal sins committed by the believer. The distinction between believers and unbelievers is not that one possesses a sin nature while the other does not. The distinction is that the believer has a new nature as well. He possesses a newborn human spirit that battles the old sin nature. Galatians 5:16-17 and Romans 7:15-25 both describe this war.

In relation to personal sin, three points should be made. First, the unbeliever is a slave to sin; he has to commit acts of sin. The believer, on the other hand, has been saved from the power of sin; he is no longer obligated to commit acts of sin (Rom. 6:1–8:13; I Jn. 1:1-2:2). Second, the believer is to reckon this fact as being true and live like it (Rom. 6:1–8:13). Third, the believer must now fight the spiritual warfare against the flesh, the devil, and the world.

In relation to imputed sin, the believer's former position of being "in Adam" is offset by his new position of being "in Messiah." For the believer, physical death is no longer the penalty for imputed sin.

Physical death is merely a means of leaving this world and entering into heaven. Furthermore, when the believer dies, his future resurrection is ensured (I Cor. 15:50-57).

## C. The Penalty for Sin in the Believer's Life

There are four possible penalties for sin in the believer's life. The first penalty is the loss of fellowship with God, as I John 1:6 shows: *If we say that we have fellowship with him and walk in the darkness, we lie, and do not the truth*. Believers belong to God's family. When they sin, they break the familial fellowship with God. According to I John 1:9, this fellowship must be restored through confession: *If we confess our sins, he is faithful and righteous to forgive us our sins, and to cleanse us from all unrighteousness*.

A second penalty for sin in the believer's life is chastisement. This is what will happen if believers fail to confess their sins. If they do not confess their sins in order to receive family forgiveness, God will chasten and discipline them. Paul made this point in I Corinthians 11:32: *But when we are judged, we are chastened of the Lord, that we may not be condemned with the world* (cf. Heb. 12:4-11).

A third possible penalty for sin in the believer's life is excommunication from the local church. This is especially true for the most heinous personal sins, those that are public and bring dishonor to the local body of believers. One such instance is found in I Corinthians 5:1-5:

> *¹It is actually reported that there is fornication among you, and such fornication as is not even among the Gentiles, that one of you has his father's wife. ²And ye are puffed up, and did not rather mourn, that he that had done this deed might be taken away from among you. ³For I verily, being absent in body but present in spirit, have already as though I were present judged him that has so wrought this thing, ⁴in the name of our Lord Yeshua, ye being gathered together, and my spirit, with the power of our Lord*

> Yeshua, ⁵to deliver such a one unto Satan for the destruction of the flesh, that the spirit may be saved in the day of the Lord Yeshua.

The public sin occurred when a member of this local congregation slept with his stepmother. This was happening with the church's knowledge, but the church was not exercising church discipline. This type of public sin dishonors a local congregation and may result in excommunication.

A fourth possible penalty for sin in the believer's life is physical death. This is a natural outcome of chastisement and excommunication if it is taken to its full extent. Previously, it was stated that physical death is no longer a penalty for believers, but rather a means of exiting this world and entering heaven. However, there is one exception to this rule. If a believer refuses to confess his or her sin after suffering a period of chastisement, the final form of chastisement may be physical death. Furthermore, if a person does not respond and repent, the natural result of excommunication is physical death inflicted upon the believer by Satan, not by the congregation. Physical death as a penalty for a believer's sins is mentioned in I Corinthians 5:5 (quoted above) and 11:28-32:

> ²⁸But let a man prove himself, and so let him eat of the bread, and drink of the cup. ²⁹For he that eats and drinks, eats and drinks judgment unto himself, if he discern not the body. ³⁰For this cause many among you are weak and sickly, and not a few sleep. ³¹But if we discerned ourselves, we should not be judged. ³²But when we are judged, we are chastened of the Lord, that we may not be condemned with the world.

The penalty of physical death will not affect the believer's salvation.

## D. The Remedy for Sin in the Believer's Life

In the believer's life, there are two types of remedies for sin: preventative remedies and applied remedies.

Regarding preventative remedies, these are intended to keep the believer from committing acts of sin. There are four such preventative remedies: meditating upon the Scriptures (Ps. 119:11); the Messiah's intercessory work (Jn. 17:15; Rom. 8:34; Heb. 7:25); the indwelling ministry of the Holy Spirit that endows the believer with the ability and power to resist sin (Jn. 7:37-39; Rom. 8:9); walking in the light of God's Word (I Jn 1:7).

Regarding applied remedies, several options are available, the first of which is self-examination (I Cor. 11:31-32). The believer is to examine himself to determine whether or not he is living in sin. If there is sin in his life, then the second remedy to apply is confession (I Jn. 1:9). The believer is to confess his sins. He is to agree with God that it is sin and is to confess his participation. Ideally, this step should be taken whenever one becomes aware of his sins.

The Bible provides two timetables with regard to applied remedies. Ephesians 4:26 teaches that confession should be made before bedtime: *Be ye angry, and sin not: let not the sun go down upon your wrath*. First Corinthians 11:27-32 emphasizes the importance of confession prior to partaking in communion.

The result of the remedy for sin in the believer's life is twofold: first, the forgiveness of personal sins; and second, the restoration of family fellowship.

Man and Sin

# Chapter IX:
# The Final Triumph over all Sin

According to the Bible, a day will come when believers achieve final victory over all sin. That day will come with the resurrection of the body. In Romans 8:23, Paul noted: *And not only so, but ourselves also, who have the first-fruits of the Spirit, even we ourselves groan within ourselves, waiting for our adoption, to wit, the redemption of our body.* In I Corinthians 15:35-49, the apostle stated:

> [35]*But some one will say, How are the dead raised? and with what manner of body do they come?* [36]*You foolish one, that which you yourself sow is not quickened except it die:* [37]*and that which you sow, you sow not the body that shall be, but a bare grain, it may chance of wheat, or of some other kind;* [38]*but God gives it a body even as it pleased him, and to each seed a body of its own.* [39]*All flesh is not the same flesh: but there is one flesh of men, and another flesh of beasts, and another flesh of birds, and another of fishes.* [40]*There are also celestial bodies, and bodies terrestrial: but the glory of the celestial is one, and the glory of the terrestrial is another.* [41]*There is one glory of the sun, and another glory of the moon, and another glory of the stars; for one star differs from another star in glory.* [42]*So also is the resurrection of the dead. It is sown in corruption; it is raised in incorruption:* [43]*it is sown in dishonor; it is raised in glory: it is sown in weakness; it is raised in power:* [44]*it is sown a natural body; it is raised a spiritual body. If there is a natural body, there is also a spiritual body.* [45]*So also it is written, The first man Adam became a living soul. The last Adam became a life-giving spirit.* [46]*Howbeit that is not first which is spiritual, but that which is natural; then that which is spiritual.*

> $^{47}$The first man is of the earth, earthy: the second man is of heaven. $^{48}$As is the earthy, such are they also that are earthy: and as is the heavenly, such are they also that are heavenly. $^{49}$And as we have borne the image of the earthy, we shall also bear the image of the heavenly.

The resurrection of the body means redemption from the body of sin because the resurrected body is free of the sin nature. For the church saints, this resurrection will occur at the rapture, some time before the tribulation. For the saints of the Hebrew Scriptures and the tribulation saints, it will occur during the seventy-five-day interval between the end of the tribulation and the start of the Messianic kingdom.[61]

When the Bible describes the final abode of all believers of all ages, it characterizes these believers as being free of sin. Hebrews 12:22-24 (cf. II Pet. 3:7–13; Rev. 20:7–22:5) describes this final dwelling place:

> $^{22}$but ye are come unto mount Zion, and unto the city of the living God, the heavenly Jerusalem, and to innumerable hosts of angels, $^{23}$to the general assembly and church of the firstborn who are enrolled in heaven, and to God the Judge of all, and to the spirits of just men made perfect, $^{24}$and to Yeshua the mediator of a new covenant, and to the blood of sprinkling that speaks better than that of Abel.

When all believers live together in the New Jerusalem upon the new earth, they will have final triumph over all sin. The church saints will achieve ultimate victory over sin even in the Messianic kingdom. However, there will be those in the kingdom with natural bodies and a sin nature. Only in the eternal order will everyone triumph over sin.

---

[61] For details regarding these eschatological things, see: Arnold G. Fruchtenbaum, *The Footsteps of the Messiah: A Study of the Sequence of Prophetic Events* (San Antonio, TX: Ariel Ministries, 2021).

# Chapter X:
# The Nature of the Law

The study of sin is meaningless if there is no law that defines what sin is. In a lawless environment, there is no sin. Hence, this concluding chapter on hamartiology will examine what the Bible teaches about the nature of the law.

## A. The Usages of the Word "Law"

In Scripture, there are six usages of the word "law." First, the majority of times that the Bible uses the term, it is in reference to the Law of Moses. Romans 6:14-15 and Galatians 4:4 are two passages that illustrate this usage:

> *[14]For sin shall not have dominion over you: for ye are not under law, but under grace. [15]What then? shall we sin, because we are not under law, but under grace? God forbid.* (Rom. 6:14-15)
>
> *but when the fulness of the time came, God sent forth his Son, born of a woman, born under the law.* (Gal. 4:4)

A second usage of the term "law" is in reference to "elemental law" or "moral law." These two expressions do not refer to specific commandments of Moses, but to the fundamental law that governs any society. Two passages illustrate this usage. The first is Romans 4:15: *for the law works wrath; but where there is no law, neither is there transgression*. This verse does not mean that there is no sin, but that there is no transgression, meaning one cannot violate a specific commandment until such a commandment is given or enacted. The second passage is Romans 5:13: *for until the law sin was in the world; but sin is not imputed when there is no law.*

A third usage of the term "law" is in reference to "civil law." Daniel 6:8 and 12 are two passages that illustrate this usage:

> *Now, O king, establish the interdict, and sign the writing, that it be not changed, according to the law of the Medes and Persians, which alters not.* (Dan. 6:8)

> *Then they came near, and spoke before the king concerning the king's interdict: Have you not signed an interdict, that every man that shall make petition unto any god or man within thirty days, save unto you, O king, shall be cast into the den of lions? The king answered and said, The thing is true, according to the law of the Medes and Persians, which alters not.* (Dan. 6:12)

A fourth usage of the word "law" is in reference to the revealed will of God. It can be seen in Psalm 119:18: *Open you my eyes, that I may behold Wondrous things out of your law.*

A fifth usage of the word "law" in Scripture is in reference to a principle of operation. This is found in Romans 7:21 and 8:2:

> *I find then the law, that, to me who would do good, evil is present.* (Rom. 7:21)

> *For the law of the Spirit of life in Messiah Yeshua made me free from the law of sin and of death.* (Rom. 8:2)

A sixth usage of the word "law" is in reference to the Law of the Messiah. Like the Law of Moses, the Law of the Messiah contains a body of specific commandments, as described in I Corinthians 9:20-21 and Galatians 6:2:

> [20]*And to the Jews I became as a Jew, that I might gain Jews; to them that are under the law, as under the law, not being myself under the law, that I might gain them that are under the law;* [21]*to them that are without law, as without law, not being without law to God, but under law to Messiah, that I might gain them that are without law.* (I Cor. 9:20-21)

*Bear ye one another's burdens, and so fulfil the law of Messiah.* (Gal. 6:2)

The term "law" appears 209 times in the New Testament, with the majority of references occurring in Romans and Galatians. Paul used the term 77 times in Romans and thirty times in Galatians.

In the New Testament alone, the term "law" is used thirteen different ways:
1. The law of *works* (Rom. 3:27)
2. The law of *faith* (Rom. 3:27)
3. The law of *God* (Rom. 7:22, 25; 8:7)
4. The law of *the mind* (Rom. 7:23)
5. The law of *sin* (Rom. 7:23, 25; 8:2)
6. The law of *the Spirit of life in Messiah Yeshua* (Rom. 8:2)
7. The law of *death* (Rom. 8:2)
8. The law of *righteousness* (Rom. 9:31)
9. The law of *Messiah* (Gal. 6:2)
10. The law of *the Jews* (Acts 25:8)
11. The law of *liberty* (Jas. 1:25; 2:12)
12. The law of *the Lord* (Lk. 2:23, 24, 39)
13. The *Law of Moses* (Lk. 2:22; 24:44; Jn. 7:23; Acts 13:39; 15:5; 28:23; I Cor. 9:9)

Although the term "law" is used in a variety of ways throughout the Scriptures, the primary reference in both testaments is to the Law of Moses.

Sin is the violation of any law that God applies to man, whether it is the moral law, the Law of Moses, or the Law of the Messiah.

## B. The Meaning of Law

The discovery of the various biblical uses of the term "law" prompts a discussion about the meaning of law. Perhaps the simplest and most straightforward definition of the term "law" as used in Scripture is that it is the expression of the divine will, enforced by power.

This straightforward definition of law has four ramifications. The first implication is that a lawgiver exists. According to the Scriptures, this Lawgiver is God. The second implication is that there is an entity that receives and must obey the law. Biblically speaking, man is the subject and is required to obey any law given by the Lawgiver as applicable to him. The third implication is that this law is an expression of the will of the lawgiver. Because in the Bible, the Lawgiver is God Himself, what He establishes as law is an expression of His divine will. The fourth implication is that the lawgiver is capable of enforcing his will. In the case of God's law, He has the power to carry out His will and may exercise His authority whenever He deems it necessary.

Having defined the term "law" and its implications, it is necessary to point out that there are two extreme views on law. One extreme is known as "antinomianism," which maintains that believers are not subject to any law. The majority of adherents of this doctrine quote verses that teach that the believer is no longer subject to the Law of Moses, which is true. However, believers continue to be bound by a law, and that is the Law of the Messiah. The second extreme is legalism. Legalism is the addition of manmade laws to God-given laws and the enactment of these manmade laws as well. Both antinomianism and legalism are incorrect. The correct balance is that the believer must obey the rules of God that apply to him in this age.

## C. Types of Law

Law is classified into two major categories: elemental law and positive enactments. In the first category, the expression "elemental law" refers to law that is incorporated into the elements, substances, and forces of rational and irrational creatures. When elemental law is wrought into the constitution of the material universe, it transforms into physical or natural laws, such as the law of gravity and the laws of thermodynamics.

Elemental law becomes moral law when it is incorporated into the constitution of rational and free beings. All humanity has some sense of morality. Even in the most inaccessible regions of the earth, people who have never been exposed to God's divine law still have some type of moral code. They retain a sense of right and wrong (Rom. 2:14-15).

There are some other aspects of elemental law. Elemental law is not arbitrary; rather, it springs from nature itself. Elemental law is not transitory; it exists as long as the elements themselves exist, whether they are rational or irrational. Elemental laws can be both negative and positive, demanding conformity to God. Even pagans have a sense of right and wrong, and they know when they have not met a certain standard. Elemental law is universal. Throughout the world, people behave as if there were a moral code.

The second category of law is positive enactments. Positive enactments are the published, written ordinances that express God's will. This is what is contained in Scripture. God's will is expressed differently in different ages or dispensations. Nevertheless, every age has a published ordinance from God.

Positive enactments are precepts expressed in three major categories. First, there are moral precepts, such as the Ten Commandments and the Sermon on the Mount. Second, there are ceremonial precepts, such as the sacrificial system of the Law of Moses and the communion service of the Law of the Messiah. Third, there are legal precepts and rules governing what is right and wrong, such as the dietary laws of the Law of Moses and the rules concerning the proper use of the spiritual gifts in the Law of the Messiah.

## D. The Purpose of the Law of God

Five points should be made regarding the purpose of God's law. First, God never gave commandments as a way of earning salvation. The purpose of the law of God, regardless of which law or which dispensation, was never to be a means of salvation (Rom. 3:20; 8:3; Gal. 3:21).

Second, the purpose of the law of God was to intensify man's knowledge of sin (Rom. 3:19-20; 5:13, 20; 7:7, 13; I Cor. 15:56; Gal. 3:19).

Third, the purpose of the law of God was to reveal the holiness of God (Rom. 7:12).

Fourth, while God's law was not intended to be a means of salvation, it was to direct man to the means of salvation, which is saving faith (Gal. 3:24).

Fifth, the purpose of the law of God is to establish a rule of life for the believer. Once a person is saved, he may ask, "How then shall I live?" "What does God expect of the believer?" "What kind of lifestyle does God want me to conduct?" The answer depends on the dispensation. Before the first coming of the Messiah, Gentile believers would follow the law codex of the Adamic and Noahic covenants. For Jewish believers, the rule of life in the Hebrew Bible was the Law of Moses. Nowadays, the rule of life for both Jewish and Gentile believers is the Law of the Messiah. However, regardless of which law it was—the law of the Adamic Covenant, the law of the Noahic Covenant, the law of the Abrahamic Covenant, the law of the Mosaic Covenant, the Law of the Messiah in the New Covenant, or the future law of the millennial system—the law of God was never given for the purpose of attaining salvation but to provide a rule of life for the believer.

## E. The Believer and the Law of God

Concerning the believer and the law of God, two simple points should be made. Simple as they are, people are very much confused about these things today and often do not know which law to follow. Sometimes they disobey commandments applicable to them and obey commandments that are not.

The first point to make is that the believer today is not bound by the Law of Moses. Gentiles were never under the Law of Moses; the Law of Moses was given only to the Jews. This means that none of the

613 commandments apply to the believer today. This truth is taught in Romans 6:14-15; 7:6; Galatians 5:18; and Hebrews 7:18-19.

The second point concerning the believer and the law of God is that the believer today is subject to the Law of the Messiah. Just as the Law of Moses contained numerous commandments, the Law of the Messiah also contains numerous commandments. Many of these commandments are the same as those found in the Law of Moses, but many others are different and sometimes contradictory to those found in the previous legal code. Therefore, it is critical to understand that believers today are not subject to the Law of Moses; they are under no obligation to obey any of the 613 commandments of this law. However, they are obligated to obey all of the commandments of the Law of the Messiah. This is taught in Romans 8:4; I Corinthians 9:20-21; Galatians 5:18; and 6:2.

In summary, believers today must be careful not to be so zealous in obeying laws that do not apply to them that they end up living in a state of disobedience to the laws and commandments that do apply to them. Disobeying a commandment of the Law of the Messiah, whether passively or actively, is to commit a sin against God.

# Chapter XI:
# Questions and Study Suggestions

Unlike in previous volumes and sections of the Come and See series, the questions and study suggestions pertaining to hamartiology are compiled into a single chapter.

***Study Suggestion:*** Memorize Romans 3:23; check box when you are sure you know it and can recite the verse from memory without having read it for at least two days: [_].

### Fill In the Blanks and Choose the Right Answers:

The expression "personal sin" refers to _____ of sin committed by _____. While the sin nature is _____, personal sin is _____; it is the act of sin. These acts of sin are committed because man is by _____ a sinner.

Personal sin is any act of sin committed by an _____ before _____ on Messiah and includes **(some / most / all)** forms of sin in daily life, whether _____ or in ignorance, which are _____ God or _____ to the character of God.

In order to define more fully all that is included in personal sin, fill in the "Could Be" section of the following chart:

| As to... | It Could Be... |
|---|---|
| Divine Requirements | Sins of |
| Object | Sins against |
| Compass | |
| "Chargeableness" | Charged to |
| Intention | |
| Sinfulness | |
| Subject | Affecting |
| God's justice | |
| Forgiveness | |
| Cause | (five things) |
| Penalty | |

In light of the Scriptures that were studied in the section on hamartiology, for each of the statements below, indicate whether the motive or mindset would render a wrong act as "sin" or "excused."

    a. What I'm doing is my business; it doesn't hurt anybody else. **(Sin / Excused)**

    b. Nobody knows I did it. **(Sin / Excused)**

    c. I had no idea; it never even crossed my mind that it might be wrong. **(Sin / Excused)**

    d. Oh, it's just a little thing, not like murder or something! **(Sin / Excused)**

    e. It's the lifestyle; it's our society; everybody does it. **(Sin / Excused)**

Regarding transmission of sin from one person to another, explain:

    a. Where acts of personal sin originate: _____

    b. The possible extent of the effect of a personal act of sin: _____

Complete the statements in the following chart:

| The Penalty | The Remedy |
|---|---|
| The penalty for personal sin is _____. | _____ God removes our _____ and _____. |
| Committing more and more personal acts of sin adds to the degree of future, eternal _____. | _____ God declares our non-_____ and adds the _____ of the Messiah to the believer. |
| The result is a state of being "_____." | The result is the of the _____ believing sinner. |

What is the purpose of studying how the Bible uses the word "law"?

By far, the major, biblical usage of the word "law" is in reference to _____.

In Psalm 119:18, where David says, "Open you my eyes, that I may behold wondrous things out of your law," the term "law" refers to the _____ of God.

Daniel 6:8 and 12 were used as examples of Civil Law. What does "Civil Law" mean?

In Romans 7:21, Paul refers to something that seems to happen over and over again (every time he wants to do good) and always has the same result (evil is present). In this sense, "law" is a _____ of _____. In American slang, a good or neutral action which consistently gets the same (bad) result is jokingly referred to as "Murphy's _____." This is what is meant by a _____ of _____.

Which two New Testament books account for more than half of the 209 usages of the word "law" in the New Testament? _____

and _____. Who is the human author of these books? _____

Without looking at your notes, try to name all 13 ways that the New Testament uses the word "law." (Hints: four of them have the word "the"; four refer to deity.) The Law of:

1. _____
2. _____
3. _____
4. _____
5. _____
6. _____
7. _____
8. _____
9. _____
10. _____
11. _____
12. _____
13. _____

The concept of "law" means: The _____ of the _____, _____ by power. This involves four implications: (a.) There is one who _____ the law, and (b.) a _____ who receives it; (c.) there is an _____ of, as well as (d.) the _____ of the divine will.

Antinomianism and legalism are the two _____ in the concept of law. Briefly explain what each term means in relation to believers:
   a. Antinomianism: _____
   b. Legalism: _____

# Questions and Study Suggestions

Give two examples of elemental laws in nature (one of which was dealt with extensively in your study of anthropology): _____ and _____.

Describe the differences between elemental law and moral law. What is moral law? _____

Name two things that elemental law is not:
1. Elemental law is not _____. Where does it originate?
2. Elemental law is not _____. How long will it exist?

Especially with regard to the moral elements, there are both _____ and _____ demands in conforming to God.

Elemental law is one type of law; what is the second type of law? _____ In what way is this second type of law an expression of God's will?

There are different codes of law for different _____. For example, that which God demanded was different before and after the _____; before and after the; and before and after the _____.

What is one thing that the law of God is not? _____

Four purposes of the law of God are:
1. To intensify man's _____ of _____.
2. To reveal the _____ of _____.
3. To lead _____ to _____.
4. To provide a _____ of _____ for the believer.

The believer today is not under the _____.
The believer today is under the _____.

CPSIA information can be obtained
at www.ICGtesting.com
Printed in the USA
BVHW030620110722
641514BV00004B/19